ALTRUISM:

MANY KINDS OF KINDNESS

Cover photo artwork by Soni S. Werner
Book design by Karin A. Childs

ISBN 10: 1936665166
ISBN 13: 978-1-936665-16-7

Altruism

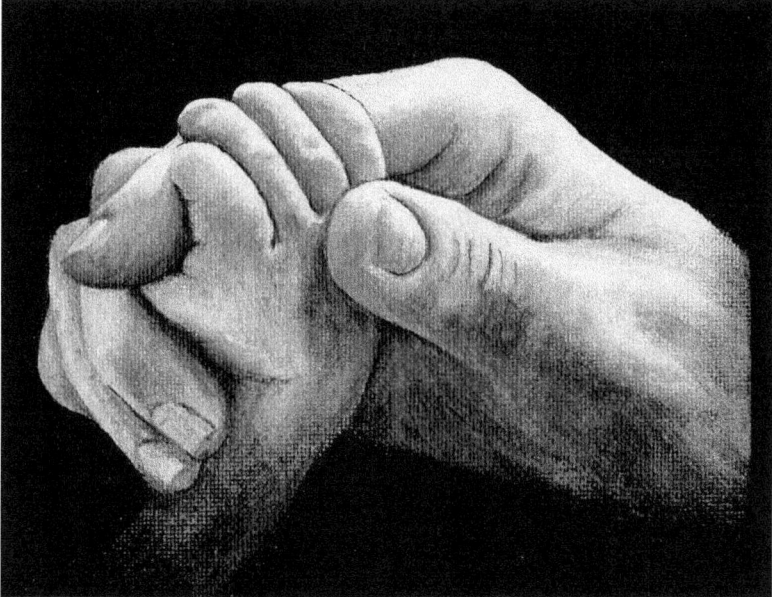

Many Kinds of Kindness

WRITTEN AND ILLUSTRATED BY
SONI S. WERNER, PH.D.

Fountain Publishing®
Rochester, Michigan

Dedicated to my parents,
Larry and Midge Soneson

Contents

Introduction

This is a resource book about altruism at two levels: kindness to body and kindness to spirit. Altruism is a word derived from the Latin and French languages, referring to other people rather than to self (egoism). So the scope of this book is about various ways that we can choose to be kind to others.

Here the reader will find the topic of human kindness to others analyzed from many different angles. There are probably dozens of ways one could organize this positive subject. The theme that was selected that holds this particular book together is about the six ways to serve others, both literally and spiritually. It is based on a well-known story from the *Holy Bible*, in the New Testament: Matthew 25:

> "For I was hungry and you gave me something to eat, I was thirsty and you gave me something to drink, I was a stranger and you invited me in, I needed clothes and you clothed me, I was sick and you looked after me, I was in prison and you came to visit me." Then the righteous will answer him, "Lord, when did we see you hungry and feed you, or thirsty and give you something to drink? When did we see you a stranger and invite you in, or needing clothes and clothe you? When did we see you sick or in prison and go to visit you?"
> The King will reply, "Truly I tell you, whatever you did for one of the least of these brothers and sisters of mine, you did for me."

Therefore, the six chapters here focus on these six ways that we are to serve our neighbor, as directed by Jesus Christ. These could be seen as six main components of altruism:

1) Serving food to the hungry
2) Serving liquids to the thirsty
3) Welcoming the stranger
4) Clothing the naked
5) Visiting the sick
6) Visiting the imprisoned

In addition to an exploration of these six literal ways that people can be altruistic to others, the scope of this book also includes explanations for what these six ways mean at a spiritual level. These ideas are derived from the theological works of the Christian scholar, Emanuel Swedenborg.

But so much could be shown about each way to be kind to others, that I have included a variety of learning modes: illustrations, true stories, examples of organizations, characters from novels, theories, psychological research about the brain, and theological concepts.

Some readers prefer stories to help them remember important ideas. Other readers prefer psychological theories and neurological research as convincing evidence. Still others have an appetite for spiritual interpretation of the meaning of Biblical verse. Using subsections with icons within the six main chapters, readers can navigate to find their preferred concepts.

Here is a key to the icons in each chapter about altruism, along with the specific purposes of these various subsections:

My story

In these sections of the chapters the reader will find short anecdotes about the author and her friends and family who have experienced various kinds of kindness, either as the helper or as the recipient of altruism.

International Altruism

These sections of the chapters include some wonderful examples of non-profit organizations that are dedicated to various human needs, such as providing food to hungry refugees around the world.

Inspirational stories

Here the reader will find examples of characters from novels that illustrate certain types of altruism. In most cases, the authors of those novels were inspired by the theological works of Emanuel Swedenborg, and they chose the genre of fiction to illustrate spiritual ideals. Some of these inspired fiction writers include: Charles Dickens, Victor Hugo, C.S. Lewis,

Alfred Lord Tennyson, Fyodor Dostoevsky, Louisa May Alcott, Henry James, and Sylvia Shaw. However, in a few cases, the stories are not fictional, but based on real people such as Helen Keller and Anne Sullivan.

Psychological theory about altruism

This symbol is a Greek letter that is pronounced psi, and stands for psychology. In these subsections of the six chapters, there is a focus on the famous psychological theory about altruism, created by Dr. Pitikin Sorokin. He was a Harvard professor of the Social Sciences. This theory has five components, so they are dealt with in the first five chapters. In the sixth chapter, there is a description of Sorokin's own story of imprisonment, which led to his analysis of human kindness in contrast to the human horrors that he witnessed.

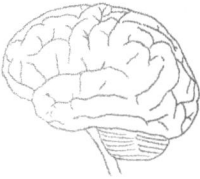

Psychological research about altruism

These subsections of the six chapters cover examples of some of the latest neuro-psychological research about altruism. In the past 30 years, research scientists have been mapping the brain and reporting their results in professional journals. This exciting research gives us clues about which brain structures are involved during altruistic thinking, feeling and behaving.

Swedenborgian perspective

This is the Greek letter theta, and here it stands for theology. In these subsections of the six chapters, the reader will find theological ideas about charity, kindness, wisdom and usefulness, according to the writings of Emanuel Swedenborg. In these books that were published over 200 years ago, Swedenborg explains the true meaning of the Bible and what it means, spiritually, to be hungry, thirsty, estranged, naked, sick and imprisoned. Those doctrines are summarized here with references to more complete quotations for those readers who wish to go into a deeper study of the theological works of Swedenborg.

Near the end of each chapter there is a chart based on doctrines derived from Swedenborg, about four degrees of charitable works. This is a unique hierarchy that emphasizes the private motives of an altruistic person, from very simple to quite sophisticated. Then examples are provided according to the topics of the six chapters: serving the hungry, thirsty, estranged, naked, sick and imprisoned.

Finally, the ends of the chapters include "Reflection Questions" for the reader to ponder when engaged in community service work. Hopefully these questions will facilitate the process of applying these various concepts to real situations.

In summary, this book is divided into six chapters based on the six ways to altruistically serve others, according to Jesus Christ. Then each chapter is divided into many subsections in order to help the reader learn about this subject from multiple viewpoints. Perhaps the varied information will solidify the reader's learning and be an inspiration to be altruistic at both the literal and the spiritual levels.

"Since the whole being or body focuses its powers primarily in the arms and hands...[and] since this is how the levels unfold and express themselves in power, the angels who are with us and are sensitive to everything in us can tell simply from a single action of our hand what we are like....

I have often been astounded by the kind of recognition angels have simply from the physical action of a hand, but it has been shown to me often enough and by personal experience.... This leads to the conclusion that the whole of charity and faith is in works and that charity and faith without works are like halos around the sun that dissipate and vanish when a cloud passes by. So time after time the Word talks about works and doing and says that our salvation depends on such things....

We should realize, though, that "works" means deeds of service that are put into action. The whole of charity and faith is in them and depends on them...."

— Emanuel Swedenborg
Divine Love and Wisdom 220

Translation by George F. Dole
©2003 by the Swedenborg Foundation, West Chester, PA

Chapter 1
What is Hunger?

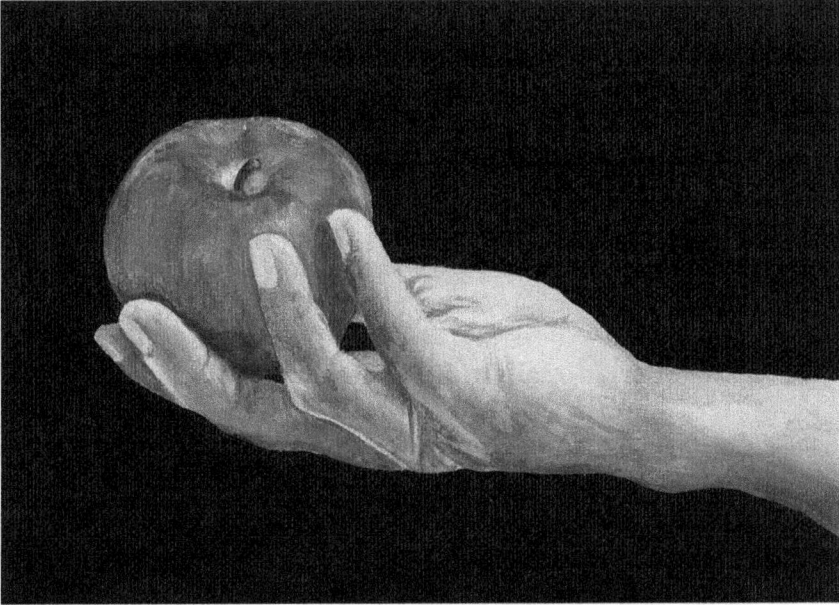

Altruism involves paying attention to what other people need, feeling empathy, and then kindly serving those needs. In this chapter the focus is on how we become aware of other people's hunger at two levels: their physical need for food and their spiritual longing for goodness. Hunger is explored through stories, examples of international organizations, a psychological theory, psychological and neurological research, and a theological explanation according to Swedenborg.

My story

Last year, I had the chance to serve a meal to 20 hungry, college students. They had spent the previous week on a service trip, voluntarily helping an organization fix up a facility that is used for social work activities. On their return trip back to campus, they stopped at my home in the mountains, which was along the way. They had worked up a good appetite and were still glowing from their successful service work. I sensed a mood of gratitude and cheerfulness. I had the fun of planning and preparing the meal, and then watching the food disappear. Even better was the activity after the meal, when their leaders guided them through a vespers service. All 20 of them sat in a big circle in our living room near the fireplace, taking turns sharing highlights of the trip. I heard them mention genuine friendship and the joy of serving others, together. We all felt the Lord's presence.

International altruism: Feeding the hungry

Too often we see headlines in the media about a disaster such as a hurricane or typhoon that wiped out a village, leaving people without food. But rarely do we see a news story about chronic hunger. It just does not make headlines because it is present everyday. There are too many people slowly dying due to malnutrition even though there is an abundance of food being produced across the globe. Recently, Danielle Nierenberg (2014) made a list of 101 organizations that are dedicated to the goal of ending world hunger. One of these altruistic organizations is called Action Against Hunger/ACF International. They are considered a leader in their efforts to address the chronic problem of malnutrition. Some of the problems that this organization addresses are delivering the food to remote people and making it affordable. (See the Appendix for the list of the other 100 altruistic organizations that are trying to address world hunger.)

Inspirational story: Feeding the hungry

Do you know the story of Little Women, by Louisa May Alcott? In this tale, Marmee, the mother of four young daughters, says to her children on Christmas morning…"Merry Christmas, little daughters! … I want to say one word before we sit down. Not far away from here lies a poor woman with a little newborn baby. Six children are huddled into one bed to keep from freezing, for they have no fire. There is nothing to eat over there, and the oldest boy came to tell me they were suffering hunger and cold. My girls, will you give them your breakfast as a Christmas present?" (Alcott, 1868, p. 14). Although at first they were reluctant to make this sacrifice, once Marmee's four daughters entered the neighbors' home, they joyfully fed all the malnourished children.

Psychological theory about altruism: Sorokin

Sorokin was a social psychologist at Harvard University in the 20th century. He studied many examples of altruism and eventually simplified his findings into a descriptive theory. He asserted that there are five dimensions of altruism that can be used to describe and explain any example of altruistic behavior. In this book, one dimension per chapter is highlighted and applied to the topic of each chapter.

The first of these five dimensions is called duration, which refers to the length of time involved in serving other people (Sorokin 1954, p.15). It could be as brief as holding the door open for a disabled friend, or as long as a lifetime commitment of adopting a disabled orphan.

In the specific example of responding to people who are chronically hungry, Sorokin would suggest that altruistic people ought to consider the duration of their commitment to help. In other words, it is more useful to try to solve the problems of hungry people over the long run, not just feeding them for today. He would applaud nonprofit organizations that figure out how families can grow their own food to feed their families. For example, this may take some long-term intervention efforts after refugees have to flee war-stricken countries, such as Syria. These refugees can only dwell in temporary camps for so long, living on food that is donated daily. Eventually, the people need to get re-established in new communities where they can organize their own food supplies (United Nations Refugee Agency, 2014). This strategy takes a longer duration of time, but may be more effective in helping people become self-sufficient after the initial urgent hunger.

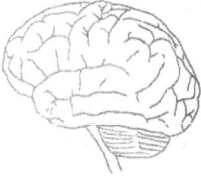

Psychological research about hunger and altruism

Many psychologists do research on people's altruistic behavior and attitudes in general, and some are specifically relevant to the case of addressing hunger. Altruistic experience actually leads to more awareness. For example, Edlefsen and Olson (2002) interviewed 17 volunteers who were helping with an emergency feeding program. They found that the more involved these volunteers were in the organization's program to feed the hungry, the more they became aware of the prevalence of hunger in their own communities. In addition, these volunteers grew in their understanding that hungry people need help to become self-sufficient in the long run, even though they may need a handout of food in the short run.

In different psychological studies about altruism researchers found that the attitude or motivations of people affect their experience of kindness. Vecina and Fernando (2013) studied over 250 volunteers of various ages, and found that there was a positive correlation between pleasure-based prosocial motivation and non-obligatory, planned helping activity that is sustained over time and within an organizational context. In other words, it is better if the volunteer feels in freedom to serve as this leads to experiencing more joy!

LaBouff and other scholars (2012) also studied the attitudes of helpful people. They found that people who are humble are much more likely to be helpful than people who are not humble. These scholars did three studies on hundreds of people, using both written assessments and behavioral reports. Even when they controlled for variables such as people trying to manage others' impressions of them, they found that humility was a consistent predictor of actual altruistic behavior.

Some psychologists investigate the workings of the brain when people are altruistic. According to several researchers at the Max Planck Institute of Neurobiology, it has recently been discovered that there is a significant place in the brain that is at the intersection of the frontal lobe, the parietal lobe and the temporal lobe. This structure of the brain is called the supramarginal gyrus, and it appears to be quite active when people are feeling empathy for others who are in some difficulty, such as feeling very hungry

(Silani, Lamm, Ruff & Singer, 2013). So, if this structure of the brain is not well developed or it has been damaged by a stroke, it is nearly impossible for them to think about the perspective of others, such as the chronically hungry. It just does not occur to them to be kind to them.

In summary, based on the findings of just these psychologists, when people make efforts to be humble this may lead to them volunteering to help others. Then if these kind people feel in freedom to join in with an organization's planned helping activity, they are more likely to experience joy while being altruistic. During the process of helping to feed hungry people, helpful people are likely to more closely pay attention to the needs of others and to feel compassion. Finally, there is scientific evidence that while people feel empathy for others who are hungry, that the supramarginal gyrus is the most active brain region involved during this experience. But if the brain is injured in that spot, empathy is hindered.

Theological perspective about spiritual hunger and altruism

According to Swedenborg, who was a Biblical scholar, there is an internal sense to the story of Matthew

25:35. Not only it is important for us to serve other people literally, such as when we are feeding the hungry, it is also important for us to serve others in a spiritual manner. People can be inspired by the Lord and the angels to figure out what others really need, spiritually, and to respond to those needs. "The angels who are with man perceive these words... for by the 'hungry' they perceive those who from affection desire good" (Swedenborg, AC 4956).

My story

I remember a time when there was a high school student in my office who seemed very hungry for goodness in his life. He was discussing whether or not to attend our college the following fall. He had already visited other colleges but there was something about the sphere here that intrigued him. I asked him to tell me about the tour he had just had that morning. He had been guided through most of the buildings, visited a class, and walked around the grounds. I asked him what impressed him the most. He paused and then he said, "I know what it is! Your mailboxes are wide open!" I was puzzled, and asked, "What do you mean?" He responded, "I want to attend a college where students respect each others' privacy and do not even touch each others' mail or graded papers which are clearly sitting in those open mailboxes! I want to attend a college and live in a community where people are actually trying to be good to each other!" He made a commitment to enroll that day, maybe because he thought that in this place he might be able to satisfy his hunger for goodness in a campus community.

Inspirational story: Feeding the spiritually hungry

Many people know the story of the grumpy old man named Ebenezer Scrooge, in *A Christmas Carol*, by Charles Dickens. He hated people who felt excitement about Christmas. But one night he had a spiritual awakening as some special spirits came to see him. When conversing with the first visiting ghost of his former work colleague, Scrooge felt very scared. He says, "Old Jacob Marley, tell me more. Speak comfort to me, Jacob!" (Dickens, 1938, p. 26). Even

18

stingy old Scrooge was hungry for words of comfort and kindness. Scrooge was just as mean as he could be, and his spiritual faith was thin, but he still had a moment of being spiritually hungry for kindness.

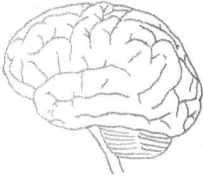

Psychological research about spiritual hunger and altruism

Psychologists not only investigate the attitudes and behavior of altruistic people when they are literally feeding the hungry. They also look deeply into the thinking patterns and motivations involved when one person helps another person who is longing for goodness. Waytz, Zaki and Mitchell (2012) are neuroscientists who know how to measure brain activity at the same moment when a person is thinking about being altruistic. They have been mapping the functions of the brain and they discovered that "activity in the dorsomedial prefrontal cortex — a region consistently involved in understanding others' mental states — predicts… time spent helping others" (Waytz, Zaki & Mitchell, 2012, p. 7646).

So, first a helpful person activates the frontal lobe while contemplating about what other people need. In addition, according to psychologists Schnall, Roper and Fessler (2010), when people witness good deeds, either in person or in a video, this prompts them to join in and also be helpful. After paying attention to others and witnessing good deeds, this can lead to a feeling of elevation, or positive mood. This sets the stage for altruistic motivation. The scholars note that this feeling of high elevation is not the same mood as just amusement or fun. In contrast, this compassionate mood is much more profound! It leads to careful altruistic behavior and the hope of wisely serving others who long to experience goodness in the world.

Swedenborgian perspective about four levels of motivation to be altruistic

While psychologists can provide clues about the mental state of an altruistic person, theology can give us an even deeper understanding about motivations. "Swedenborg distinguishes natural compassion from genuine charity, indicating that genuine charity requires looking with discernment to the quality of each neighbor.   In Swedenborg's view, each person is the neighbor according to the quality of that person's good. ...When acting in charity, good love blends compassion with justice and discernment, and takes different forms depending on the different needs of each neighbor. Each neighbor is recognized equally, but a different treatment may be directed toward each neighbor's good " (Klein, 1998, p. 82; see also Swedenborg TCR 406- 419, 428, AC 1419, 6703-6712, 6812-6824; *Charity* 72-89; HH 268).

Rev. Dr. Ted Klein is a Swedenborgian scholar who has focused much of his work on applying these doctrines to situations of social injustice. He highlights both the spiritual growth of people in need as well as the people who come forward to kindly help. He asserts that it is through these challenging encounters with each other that people have the opportunity to redefine themselves and come closer to God. "In regeneration, we can gradually come into a life of love, wisdom, and use in connection with the world" (Klein, 1998, p. 43).

Swedenborg tells us that there are four levels of charity, from simple helpfulness to more complex discernment (AC 3688). It takes more mental effort and focus to discern what others really need at the more sophisticated levels. Here is a paraphrased summary of the four levels of the motives of a helpful person, first with examples of feeding the hungry literally, and then with examples of helping people who are spiritually hungry for goodness.

FOUR LEVELS OF CHARITY	EXAMPLES OF FEEDING THE HUNGRY
Level 1) Simply give to others from the heart, so as to get a reward in heaven.	A person hands out food to anyone who is hungry and hopes for a heavenly reward.
Level 2) Gives to anyone who is in distress, with no distinction about whether the receivers will use the contributions for good or ill.	A person gives food to hungry people but may be shocked if a recipient uses it for evil purposes.
Level 3) Gives only to people that are thought to be upright (but may stereotype people).	A person only gives food to those groups of people judged to be good, overall.
Level 4) Searches for what is good in anyone and supports that component; sees the Lord within a person and is altruistic to that part. If this is done with a full heart and with acknowledgement that all goodness comes from the Lord, this person is regenerate.	A person searches for positive aspects of people, and gives them food with no thought of reward.

FOUR LEVELS OF CHARITY	EXAMPLES OF SPIRITUALLY FEEDING THE HUNGRY WITH GOODNESS
Level 1) Simply give to others from the heart, so as to get a reward in heaven.	A person hands out kindness to anyone, and hopes for a heavenly reward.
Level 2) Gives to anyone who is in distress, with no distinction about whether the receivers will use the contributions for good or ill.	A person gives kindness and support to spiritually hungry people but may be shocked if a recipient uses it for evil purposes.
Level 3) Gives only to people that are thought to be upright (but may stereotype people).	A person only gives kindness to those groups of people judged to be good, overall.
Level 4) Searches for what is good in anyone and supports that component; sees the Lord within a person and is altruistic to that part. If this is done with a full heart and with acknowledgement that all goodness comes from the Lord, this person is regenerate.	A person searches for positive aspects of people, and gives them kindness with no thought of reward.

In the next chapter the focus turns to how people can be altruistic to others who are thirsty, both literally and spiritually.

Reflecting on your community service experiences:
1) Sorokin describes five dimensions of altruism, including duration of time. What is the length of time you have helped in this community project? Do you plan to continue?
2) Have you asked one of the other volunteers there about how long he/she has been doing community service there? What did you learn about this person?
3) Why does this community service work need to be done? Who benefits?
4) Describe your expectations about doing community service work when you first started.
5) Does this community service work involve preventing a problem, or intervening in an ongoing problem, or rehabilitating a more serious situation?

Chapter 2
What is Thirst?

Altruism involves paying attention to what other people need, feeling empathy, and then kindly serving those needs. In this chapter the focus is on how we become aware of other people's thirst at two levels: their physical need for liquids and their spiritual longing for truth. Thirst is explored through stories, examples of international organizations, a psychological theory, psychological and neurological research, and a theological explanation according to Swedenborg.

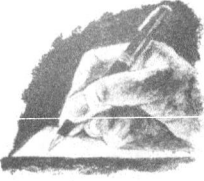

My story

One of my relatives lives close to where an international marathon occurs each spring. Every year, she and her children gather up paper cups and jugs of water and head out to the sidewalk along the route of the marathon. It is with great delight that they hand cups of fresh water to the hundreds of runners as they go streaming by. My relatives will never know the names of each runner, but they love providing liquids to these brave, thirsty runners who physically challenge themselves to run for miles. I can just picture people reaching out with cups of water to hundreds of runners, who do not stop, but drink while they run! These acts of kindness are done with no expectation of a "thank-you", or even recognition by a local news reporter. They love to give water to thirsty people, just when it is needed most.

International Altruism: Serving water to the thirsty

There are some amazing altruistic people who organize meetings and establish policies and procedures regarding the provision of clean water to the thirsty around the world. In 1992, the United Nations held a conference about the environment and development. One issue that they addressed was the serious problem of the shortage of clean water for human consumption. Over one third of the people on the planet struggle with finding clean water each day. Now over 20 years later, the World Water Council, established in response to the United Nations recommendation, is still in existence addressing this issue. The group includes 300 organizations from 40 countries who "promote awareness of critical water issues at all levels, including the highest decision-making level, to facilitate efficient conservation, protection, development, planning, management, and use of water in all its dimensions on an environmentally sustainable basis for the benefit of all life on earth" (World Water Council, 2014. See the Appendix for more examples of organizations dedicated to addressing world thirst).

Inspirational stories: Serving water to the thirsty

Deserts have a scarcity of water and tribal groups in the Middle East often fight to the death over the rights to wells. This conflict is illustrated in an award winning film entitled *Lawrence of Arabia*. Lawrence had been a British office who participated in political conflicts across the desert region during World War I. Many times Lawrence rode on a camel across miles of hot, sandy terrain and when he arrived at his destination his first urgent craving was always for water. Sometimes, if his hosts were friendly, they satisfied his thirst by handling him a jug of fresh water. But not everyone he met in the desert was altruistic. Unfortunately, some desert dwellers tortured their enemies with water deprivation (Wilson, 1992).

Psychological theory about altruism: Sorokin

Sorokin was the social psychologist mentioned in Chapter 1 who studied many examples of altruism and eventually simplified his findings into a descriptive theory. He asserted that there are five dimensions of altruism, focusing mostly on the helper. In Chapter 1, there is a description of one of the dimensions called duration. Another one of these five dimensions is called extensivity (Sorokin 1954, p.15). Sorokin felt that love for humanity could range from only focusing on oneself (egoism) all the way to loving the entire universe (altruism). He encouraged people to not only be altruistic to those in their immediate clan but to also reach out to people who are different in terms of gender, race, ethnicity, location, economic level, and so forth. This effort to assist people who are distant or quite different from oneself indicates the extent of altruistic extensivity.

In the specific case of dealing with chronic thirst across the globe, Sorokin would suggest that the altruistic individuals of an organization should consider the scope of their efforts in terms of extensivity. In other words, altruistic individuals who direct philanthropic organizations ought to broaden their missions to help people who are thirsty throughout the world, and not just in one's own household. If he was still alive Sorokin would have appreciated the current work of the World Water Council and their efforts to collect philanthropic donations and arrange for distribution of clean water to people far and wide. Sorokin was concerned that too often people just take care of their own family members and neighbors and do not devote their resources to people of different cultures.

Of course, it is not practical for each person who has plenty of water to get on a plane carrying a bucket, and then visit thirsty people in far away places. So we need a system of nonprofit organizations to gather funds and work on our behalf to address this problem of chronic thirst for clean water, extensively, beyond our own kitchens. The World Water Council members demonstrate a high degree of extensivity as they continuously arrange for the distribution of potable water across the globe, wherever people need it the most. The staff and volunteers who choose to work in this effort must have adjusted their psychological scope to care about people far away, even if they never met them.

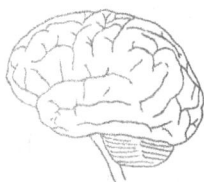

Psychological research about thirst and altruism

Some psychologists have been investigating how community service experiences relate to people's deeper reflections and religious maturity. They address questions such as: is it the experience that leads to the thoughtful reflection, or the other way around? Is there any connection between a person's religiosity and their volunteer service work? Here are just a few examples of these types of studies, some of which are focused on serving thirsty people.

Many young adults and adolescents feel called to do what they can to help people in need. Some college and high school faculty arrange for their students to volunteer in social service agencies serving milk, coffee and soup to homeless people. In 1994, Yates analyzed the reflections of 160 young people who did this type of altruistic work in soup kitchens. The youth served the homeless people for a couple hours a week for a year, and their attitudes changed over time. Yates gave the young people questionnaires, and she also asked to read their reflective essays. She found that the young people were "(1) examining preconceptions about homeless people, (2) comparing one's life situation to another's, and (3) evaluating justice and responsibility" (Yates,

1995, p. 2908). In addition, she found that "feeling good about helping and learning about the life of a person served were associated with more encompassing reflections" (Yates, 1995, p. 2908). It appears that even if the young people did not personally know the homeless people to whom they served liquids, the experience stimulated their deeper thoughts about why anyone becomes homeless and has difficulty getting their needs met. Altruistic service experiences led to young people having deeper thoughts about justice in the world.

In a different psychological study about altruistic young adults who get involved in service work, Bernt (1989) investigated the development of religious maturity. He assumed that people who are oriented towards extrinsic religion are less mature than people who are oriented towards intrinsic religion. In other words, children are taught by their elders to practice their religion by attending church (extrinsically motivated), but as people become more mature, they begin to think for themselves and wonder how to really live their religion (intrinsically motivated).

Bernt studied 245 young adults who were just about to finish undergraduate college and at the time of life when people might develop from a state of extrinsically motivated religion to more intrinsically motivated religion. The psychologist found that the college students who had voluntarily applied to do year-long service trips right after college were much more likely to be more religiously mature (more intrinsically motivated) than the students who did not apply to go on service trips. Perhaps these young people had developed beyond just religious obedience and memorization of scripture, to a more mature level of applying their religion to life.

Therefore, when adolescents and young adults get involved in serving other people on a weekly basis, such as providing liquids to homeless people, this experience helps them reflect deeply and empathize with others. This deeper reflection stimulated by community service work might help young people to become more spiritually mature. Then, when given the chance to offer to do altruistic trips of a longer duration, they might be the first to sign up.

Theological perspective about spiritual thirst and altruism

When a person desires truth from affection, this is what is meant by spiritual thirst (Swedenborg, AC 4956). In other words, people have strong feelings that can lead to them becoming curious about life. It makes them wonder and ask important questions. Some will even go on a quest to search for truth, which they can apply to their lives.

"People who look to the Lord, turn from what is harmful, and do their daily work sincerely, justly, and faithfully become embodiments of charity. A conscientious approach to work is central to Swedenborg's concept that the life of charity combines a spiritual awareness with an active life in the world....A truly charitable life involves acting honestly and fairly out of an inward spiritual motivation. In this, there is a joining together of genuine love, spiritual insights, and actions with good consequences" (Klein, 1998, p. 35; see also Swedenborg *Charity* 158 and HH 535).

My story

Spiritual thirst can lead people to eagerly search for important ideas about life. I love the story about a colleague who had just gotten married. He and his wife were deeply in love, but they were not satisfied with the way love was portrayed in the movies and novels. So they decided to go to the library and search for wisdom about true marriage love. In their spiritual quest for truth, they discovered a book written 250 years ago, called *Conjugial Love*, by Swedenborg. They were delighted with the description of marriage in heaven, and how people can prepare for this state by the way they live their lives on earth. Now, decades later, my colleague has become a minister and college professor teaching religion. On some days, his wife joins him as they co-teach young people about the ideals of marriage love. Their spiritual thirst, which was an affectionate search for true ideas that could help them in their marriage, led them on their quest. Now they altruistically help the next generation who are thirsty for truth about how to find happiness in their relationships.

Inspirational story: Quenching spiritual thirst

Have you ever heard of the story of *The Portrait of a Lady*, by Henry James? This story illustrates an intellectual and spiritual thirst. It was written over a century ago, but it is still read by many English majors in college, today. The main character in *The Portrait of a Lady* was a woman named Isabel Archer, who was described as having "an immense curiosity about life, and was constantly staring and wondering" (James, 1881, p. 45). She seemed incredibly thirsty for knowledge and adventure, and when faced with difficult personal circumstances, she was always searching for the right thing to do. Isabel Archer is similar to any of us when we feel a great longing for fresh new ideas, a moral compass, or some guiding principle to help us live our lives.

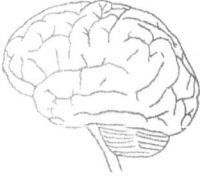

Psychological research about spiritual thirst and altruism

People often want to help quench each other's thirst for ideas. According to the Asian psychologists named Chang and Chuang (2011), even when people do not see each other face-to-face there is a human desire to share knowledge. The internet provides a wonderful opportunity for knowledge sharing in a virtual community. Writers and readers are both thirsty for knowledge and eager to share what they know even when there is no payment or reward for such sharing.

Based on a survey of knowledge-sharers in a virtual community, altruistic motivation had a significant effect on knowledge sharing. "Reputation, social interaction, and trust had positive effects on the quality, but not the quantity, of shared knowledge" (Chang & Chaung, 2011, p. 9). The psychologists also found that knowledge sharers tended to value reciprocity, or the idea of both giving and receiving knowledge, on the internet. This is called reciprocal altruism. Baytiyeh & Pfaffman (2010) found similar results when they studied people who voluntarily contribute their knowledge to the internet in open source software. Based on a survey of over 70 volunteers, people had the "desire to help for the greater good worldwide" (p. 1345), so they repeatedly shared knowledge and tools in their virtual communities.

Whether people are thirsty for practical facts or ideal truths, it is remarkable how often they are motivated to learn all they can and then altruistically share what they know.

Swedenborgian perspective about four levels of motivation to be altruistic

Altruism can be analyzed according to behaviors, thoughts, feelings and motivations. The theological perspective emphasizes the private motives of people while they are planning and doing acts of kindness. While it is often difficult to tell what another person is pondering through observation, it is useful for each of us to be aware of our own motives. Hopefully we become more sincere and effective as we mature, but there is no guarantee. Spiritual maturation is a choice. According to Swedenborg, it is wise to pay very close attention to the people we are serving at any moment.

Then we can be more effective as we attempt to serve them, bringing out the best in our neighbors. In the case of addressing spiritual thirst, we ought to listen carefully to what others want to know before sharing what we believe to be true.

"Swedenborg distinguishes natural compassion from genuine charity, indicating that genuine charity requires looking with discernment to the quality of each neighbor. In Swedenborg's view, each person is the neighbor according to the quality of that person's good. ...When acting in charity, good love blends compassion with justice and discernment, and takes different forms depending on the different needs of each neighbor. Each neighbor is recognized equally, but a different treatment may be directed toward each neighbor's good" (Klein, 1998, p. 82; see also Swedenborg TCR 406- 419, 428, AC 1419, 6703-6712, 6812-6824; *Charity* 72-89; HH 268).

Swedenborg tells us that there are four levels of charity, from simple helpfulness to more complex discernment (AC 3688). Although it may be hard to figure out what others truly need, it is important to try. Then we can discern what others really need at the more sophisticated levels. Here is a paraphrased summary of the four levels of the motives of a helpful person, first with examples of providing liquids for the thirsty literally, and then with examples of helping people who are spiritually thirsty for truth.

FOUR LEVELS OF CHARITY	EXAMPLES OF GIVING WATER TO THE THIRSTY
Level 1) Simply give to others from the heart, so as to get a reward in heaven.	A person hands out drinks to anyone and hopes for a heavenly reward.
Level 2) Gives to anyone who is in distress, with no distinction about whether the receivers will use the contributions for good or ill.	A person gives out drinks to people but may be shocked if a recipient uses it for evil purposes.
Level 3) Gives only to people that are thought to be upright (but may stereotype people).	A person only gives liquids to those groups of people judged to be good, overall.
Level 4) Searches for what is good in anyone and supports that component; sees the Lord within a person and is altruistic to that part. If this is done with a full heart and with acknowledgement that all goodness comes from the Lord, this person is regenerate.	A person searches for positive aspects of people, and hands out liquids with no thought of reward.

FOUR LEVELS OF CHARITY	EXAMPLES OF SPIRITUALLY GIVING WATER TO THE THIRSTY WITH TRUTH
Level 1) Simply give to others from the heart, so as to get a reward in heaven.	A person hands out truth to anyone, and hopes for a heavenly reward.
Level 2) Gives to anyone who is in distress, with no distinction about whether the receivers will use the contributions for good or ill.	A person gives truth to spiritually thirsty people but may be shocked if a recipient uses it for evil purposes.
Level 3) Gives only to people that are thought to be upright (but may stereotype people).	A person only gives truth to those groups of people judged to be good, overall.
Level 4) Searches for what is good in anyone and supports that component; sees the Lord within a person and is altruistic to that part. If this is done with a full heart and with acknowledgement that all goodness comes from the Lord, this person is regenerate.	A person searches for positive aspects of people, and gives them truth with no thought of reward.

In the next chapter the focus turns to how people can be altruistic to others who are feeling like strangers, both literally and spiritually.

Reflecting on your community service experiences:

1) Sorokin described five dimensions of altruism, and one of them is extensivity. Describe how similar or different the people are from you in this community service setting: age, gender, background, race, religion, and so forth. How do you feel about working with people who are extensively different from you?

2) What skills do you need to strengthen so you can be even more effective in your service work?

3) Are you doing service work that deals with hunger or thirst, literally?

4) Are you doing service work that addresses anyone's hunger for goodness or thirst for ideas?

Chapter 3
What is a Stranger?

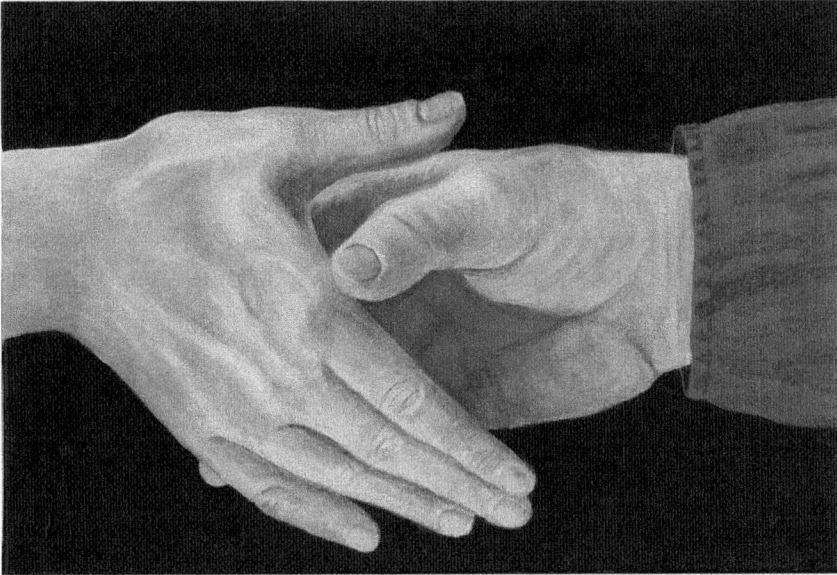

Altruism involves paying attention to what other people need, feeling empathy, and then kindly serving those needs. In this chapter the focus is on how we become aware of other people's estrangement at two levels: their literal need to be welcomed in a strange land, and their eagerness for assistance on their spiritual journeys. Estrangement is explored through stories, examples of international organizations, a psychological theory, psychological and neurological research, and a theological explanation according to Swedenborg.

My story

At our college, we have students who apply to be College Ambassadors. If selected, they become cheerful tour guides who have the responsibility of welcoming teenagers to campus. These strangers on the tours want to know about whether to come attend our college the following fall. I have watched these enthusiastic Ambassadors give the campus tours to shy visitors, who brought their parents or friends along for moral support. The loyalty to this college that these Ambassadors express during their tours is a joy to experience. Even if the visitors act reserved during the tour, they later inform us that it was the evident love for this college and the genuine interest in them as future students that convinced them that this could be a welcoming place. The Admissions Office staff knows that it is this enthusiastic welcoming of strangers that is often a deciding factor in the college selection process.

International altruism: Welcoming the stranger

The American Psychological Association decided to start a task force with members appointed by their president, to improve the advocacy of immigrants (Suarez-Orozco, 2011). The helpful people on this task force are focused on improving the dialogue between people who provide care for immigrants and those that do research on this population. The members of the task force are also communicating directly with the refugee efforts of the United Nations, by raising awareness of the psychological needs of these children, adults and elders who had to leave their homes and get resettled, due to political conflicts. These immigrants are estranged and need to be welcomed into new communities. (See the Appendix for more information about organizations that are welcoming strangers).

Inspirational story: Welcoming the stranger

It is not unusual to find a story with the theme of a stranger encountering a community where conflict occurs. Many people have seen the Broadway play based on the novel *Les Miserables*, by Victor Hugo (1862). The main character, Jean

Vanjean was taken up as a thief when he stole bread for his starving relatives, in France in the 1800's. After serving nineteen years in prison, Jean Vanjean is free but avoided by a populace suspicious of any ex-convict on parole. The kindly Bishop Myriel welcomes this stranger and lets him stay for the night at the church rectory, but Valjean takes advantage of this kindness and steals the church silver. He is caught by the police who accuse him of theft, once again. But the Bishop gives him even more silver and says that, "… his life has been spared for God, and that he should use money from the silver candlesticks to make an honest man of himself" (Hugo, 1862). Jean Vanjean does turn his life around and altruistically serves an entire community for decades. Bishop Myriel was remarkably forgiving, and he can serve as a role model to us all as we try to welcome strangers and help them on their journeys.

Psychological theory about altruism: Sorokin

Sorokin was the social psychologist mentioned in earlier chapters who studied many examples of altruism and eventually simplified his findings into a descriptive theory with five dimensions. Previously, we discussed the dimensions of extensivity and duration of altruistic behavior. Another one of Sorokin's five dimensions is called purity. This has more to do with a helpful person's rationale or purpose. Observers may not always be able to tell the extent of purity of another person's intentions, but each person can honestly reflect on his/her own motives when doing an altruistic action. Even if it is abstract, purity is an essential dimension of altruism and it is useful to encourage volunteers to reflect on why people do what they do. Purity can range from self-centered hopes for service awards, to sincere desires to detect what others need and then serving with a generous heart. Sorokin believed that an altruistic person's purity of motive was enhanced when he/she had a deep belief in God (Sorokin 1954, p.15).

While it is sometimes obvious that less mature people may be helpful to others for egotistical reasons such as asking for applause, Sorokin encouraged everyone to strive for more pure motives. Purity is an aspect of altruism that is much more difficult to assess in contrast to duration, which can be measured in the hours, weeks or days that a person is helpful. Purity is also more difficult to quantify compared to extensivity, which could be calculated in terms of the miles between one's home and the location of the community that received donated dollars.

In spite of the difficulties involved in measuring purity, people can choose to make a conscious effort to shift their private motives from a longing for honors to a more sincere desire to help others. So in the specific case of the altruistic act of welcoming strangers, this involves developing compassion for the strangers' plight and then generously acting to bring those people into the group with no selfish interests in mind.

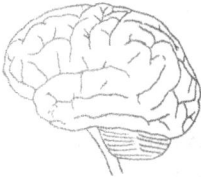

Psychological research about strangers and altruism

Even though it is a challenge to assess the purity of motives experienced when people help strangers, psychologists do try. The following studies involve quantitative investigations into the effects of mindful meditation on attitudes towards strangers, and forgiveness and empathy for friends vs. strangers.

Rangan and his colleagues (2013) conducted an online study done involving over 2,000 people who practice one of the following mindfulness traditions: Tibetan and Theravada Buddhist meditation, centering prayer, yoga or secular mindfulness. Compared to other people who do not practice any of these contemplative activities, these meditation practitioners experienced many psychological benefits, including a compassionate attitude towards strangers. The more intensely a person practiced his/her tradition, the more he/she experienced a kind attitude towards unknown people. Also those meditation practitioners who engaged in other-focused mindful routines that were also religion-based were significantly more altruistic than those who practiced self-focused, secular mindfulness.

In another psychological study that concerned attitudes towards strangers, Baumgartner and other neuroscientists (2012) were engaged in mapping the brain activity during the moments when people are experiencing certain altruistic thoughts. In their research they discovered that certain parts of the brain are involved in parochial altruism, which is the "preference for altruistic behavior towards in-group members and mistrust or hostility towards out-group members" (Baumgartner et al, 2012, p. 1452). They arranged for fMRI assessments of the brain activity of research participants, and concluded that people are usually more lenient when punishing in-group members for social norm violations, compared to when they pass judgment on out-group members (strangers).

During this action of being more lenient, these participants were more neurally active in their dorsomedial prefrontal cortex and bilateral temporo-parietal junction as if they were looking for ways to justify their lenient attitudes towards people with whom they were most familiar. In contrast, these same participants used different structures of their brains when harshly punishing out-group members, who were strangers to them. This research means that there may be a tendency for people to be highly suspicious of strangers and to punish them more harshly if there is a violation of a social norm, not even looking for a justification for those transgressions. This makes altruism to strangers all the more remarkable, since people must overcome this tendency to be suspicious and judgmental of out-group members in order to want to be kind to them at all.

In a different study that explored human reactions to strangers, that also involved assessments of brain activity, Meyer and her colleagues (2013) analyzed empathy for strangers compared with empathy for friends. These neuroscientists set up an experiment in which participants in the study were led to believe that other people were suffering due to being socially excluded. They found that when participants observed a close friend being left out socially, the same structures of the brain were active as when the participants themselves experienced painful social rejection: the ACC (anterior cingulate cortex) and the insula. She writes, "alternatively, observing a stranger's exclusion activated regions associated with thinking about the traits, mental states and intentions of others" (Meyer et al, 2013, p. 446). These neural structures are mostly in the frontal lobe where people do their rational thinking, rather than experiencing emotional empathy.

Reactions towards strangers occurred in the form of thoughts more than feelings. These neuroscientists concluded that it is quite normal for people to immediately feel emotional compassion for the pain of others whom they already know and love. However, it is more common for people to experience some emotional distance when contemplating the social pain of strangers, and so they focus more on their dispassionate thoughts.

Just based on these three recent studies about how people relate to strangers, it seems that it is quite common for people to initially judge strangers' social mistakes quite harshly, and to experience emotional distance when they understand that strangers are in pain from social rejection. However, through contemplative, religious practices such as mindful meditation or prayer, people can actually increase their compassionate attitude and behavior towards strangers.

Theological perspective about spiritual strangers and altruism

Swedenborg offers an internal sense to what it means to be a stranger. At this deeper level, a stranger is anyone who is on a journey and unsure of what to do next in life. There is a loss of direction and purpose. "The stranger is one who is willing to be instructed" (Swedenborg AC1463, 4958, 6004:3e). We are told that it would be unkind to take advantage of this type of stranger. This

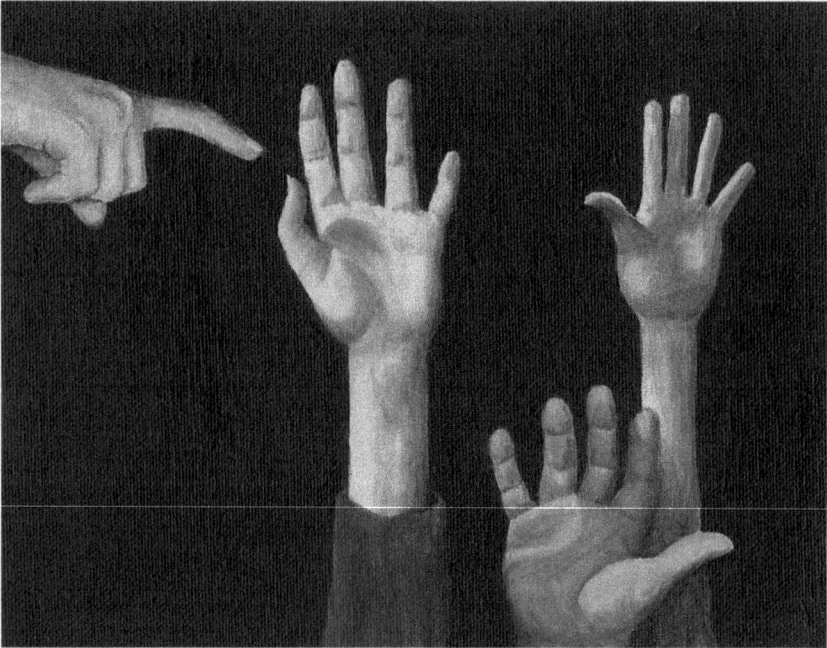

person is in our world needing guidance about how to live a better life. These spiritual strangers are eagerly asking questions, and we have the opportunity to be kind by showing them how and why to live a good life; but first we need to care about them. Sojourners are wanting to know what is good and true (Swedenborg, AE 223:15). They may already know how to live a moral and civil life, but may still be wondering about how to be a more spiritual person (Swedenborg, AC 2115, 2915, 2496).

While spiritually thirsty people seek truths, spiritual sojourners want to know how to apply truths to life (Swedenborg, AC 1896, AC 8890). We are taught that angels are very good at instructing spiritual sojourners initially with introductory ideas, and then later with deeper truths, all in the hopes of guiding sojourners on how to lead a spiritually good life (Swedenborg, AC 1463). Apparently, we should not give sojourners truths that are too internal at first, but give them external, tangible ideas to start with. We should treat strangers with respect and with the same attitude that we would treat people we have known for a long time (Swedenborg, AC 9195, AC 9268). Like the Good Samaritan, we should help strangers who are injured by giving them oil (which represents kindness), give them wine (which represents truth), and provide a place for them to rest and recover (Swedenborg AE 375). We should never take advantage of strangers by teaching them false ideas or leading them astray. We were all learners at certain points, so it is important to have empathy for those people who are strangers seeking to learn today.

My story

Recently I heard about a college student who wrote about how grateful he was for his advisor who helped him when he needed it the most. After spending a year feeling rather lost and without direction, on his last day at the college he wrote, "This whole time that I have been confused on what to do and where to go with my life, she has been my number one cheerleader, friend, advisor, motivator, and she has not stopped to take a breath once. The one large conclusion that I came to was that her unconditional love has no bounds and she will not stop till she finds a way to make whatever it is you want done happen. I can't thank her enough and I will miss her for everything she has done for me. I know without her, I don't think I would have even made the step to find a new life path" (Anonymous, personal communication, 2014). This advisor offered just the right answers to this advisee's questions, to help him on his journey. She nurtured this spiritual stranger.

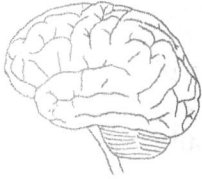

Psychological research about spiritual strangers and altruism

In some ways, young adults are like strangers that older people should carefully guide. But how can they guide young people to learn how to take up the mantle and, in turn, reach out to other strangers? Psychologists have been investigating how to guide adolescents so that they will become altruistic to both literal strangers and spiritual strangers. For instance, Grossman and Garry (1997) published a summary of the activities of the Big Brother/Big Sister program that is active across the USA. "Its mission is to make a difference in the lives of young people, primarily through a professionally supported one-to-one relationship with a caring adult, and to assist them in reaching their highest potential as they grow into responsible men and women by providing committed volunteers, national leadership, and standards of excellence" (Grossman & Garry, 1997, p. 7). These authors evaluated the effectiveness of these nurturing relationships and concluded that even though the Big Brothers and Sisters started out as strangers to the young people assigned to them, important relationships developed.

In another study, which took place in Hong Kong, adolescents were involved in a training program to not only receive guidance from caring adults, but to learn how to reach out to strangers themselves. Cheung (2006) found that it was critical to engage young people in experiential learning programs so they can learn how to be altruistic. He conducted an experiment comparing adolescents who were given experiential learning opportunities by advisors with those adolescents who were not involved in service work. "Those who volunteered for services to new immigrants, to people with mental retardation, and to chronic patients had significantly higher voluntarism levels than others" (Cheung, 2006, p. 57).

Thus, not only do young people need guidance for their own

life journeys, they also need to be taught how to be altruistic to strangers. They need to be given realistic opportunities to reach out to strangers, such as immigrants to their countries. This helps them become socially responsible adults and be useful members of society.

Swedenborgian perspective about four levels of motivation to be altruistic

The theological perspective of altruism addresses what Sorokin called purity. While Sorokin did acknowledge that there is a range of pure motives from egotistical to selfless, he did not provide more detail than that. Swedenborg's theological perspective contributes an entirely unique model for describing the range of purity. In his writings, there is an emphasis on paying attention to both the subtle differences of other people in need and one's own reasons for helping. In the dual cases of literally assisting strangers who want to become accepted into a community or responding to questions of people on their spiritual journeys, this model can be especially useful.

"Each person we encounter is a neighbor to be loved, but our practice of charity must be attuned to the nature of each neighbor. We may find one person so trustworthy that we would trust that person with our life. Another person's actions may give us good reason not to trust. ...Our treatment of each neighbor should depend on the quality of each neighbor's treatment of others. We need to be prudent and discriminating in our practice of charity, guarding against unintentionally contributing to harm, and continually seeking the best way to love and respond to each individual" (Klein, 1998, p. 37; see also Swedenborg *Charity* 51, 52, 55, and AC 6703, 6704, 6818).

Dr. Wilson van Dusen was a Swedenborgian scholar and a psychiatrist. He took an interdisciplinary approach when he wrote about how people can be pure and kind in their paid work or volunteer activities, which Swedenborg called uses. He wrote, "uses is a way of speaking to all there is. It is a spiritual communication. You wish to speak to God? Do the task at hand with the greatest faithfulness and devotion. I must emphasize, any task" (van Dusen, 2000, p. 38-39).

"Swedenborg distinguishes natural compassion from genuine charity, indicating that genuine charity requires looking with discernment to the quality of each neighbor. In Swedenborg's view, each person is the neighbor according to the quality of that person's good. ...When acting in charity, good love blends compassion with justice and discernment, and takes different forms depending on the different needs of each neighbor. Each neighbor is recognized equally, but a different treatment may be directed toward each neighbor's good" (Klein, 1998, p. 82; see also Swedenborg TCR 406- 419, 428, AC 1419, 6703-6712, 6812-6824; *Charity* 72-89; HH 268).

As in previous chapters, the four levels of charity can be applied to the example of this chapter: literally and spiritually serving the strangers and sojourners in our lives (Swedenborg, AC 3688: 3-5).

FOUR LEVELS OF CHARITY	EXAMPLES OF WELCOMING STRANGERS
Level 1) Simply give to others from the heart, so as to get a reward in heaven.	A person welcomes any stranger and hopes for a heavenly reward.
Level 2) Gives to anyone who is in distress, with no distinction about whether the receivers will use the contributions for good or ill.	A person welcomes any stranger but may be shocked if a recipient uses it for evil purposes.
Level 3) Gives only to people that are thought to be upright (but may stereotype people).	A person only welcomes groups of strangers judged to be good, overall.
Level 4) Searches for what is good in anyone and supports that component; sees the Lord within a person and is altruistic to that part. If this is done with a full heart and with acknowledgement that all goodness comes from the Lord, this person is regenerate.	A person searches for positive aspects of strangers, and welcomes them with no thought of reward.

FOUR LEVELS OF CHARITY	EXAMPLES OF SPIRITUALLY WELCOMING STRANGERS BY ANSWERING THEIR QUESTIONS
Level 1) Simply give to others from the heart, so as to get a reward in heaven.	A person responds to questions of instruction about life to anyone, and hopes for a heavenly reward.
Level 2) Gives to anyone who is in distress, with no distinction about whether the receivers will use the contributions for good or ill.	A person responds to questions of instruction about life but may be shocked if a recipient uses it for evil purposes.
Level 3) Gives only to people that are thought to be upright (but may stereotype people).	A person only responds to questions of instruction about life from people judged to be good, overall.
Level 4) Searches for what is good in anyone and supports that component; sees the Lord within a person and is altruistic to that part. If this is done with a full heart and with acknowledgement that all goodness comes from the Lord, this person is regenerate.	A person searches for positive aspects of people, and responds to their questions of instruction about life with no thought of reward.

In the next chapter, the focus will turn to offering kindness to people who are literally and spiritually needing protective clothing.

Reflecting on your community service experiences:
1) Sorokin described five dimensions of altruism, and one of them is purity. Are you aware of your own motives for doing community service work? Initially you may have signed up so you can get the reward of college credit, but have you noticed any shift in your motivation since then?
2) Were you a stranger when you first arrived at this community service setting? What did that feel like to be welcomed into the organization?
3) Have you had a chance to welcome any other new people, so that they feel like they belong?
4) Have you ever helped some new person, in any setting, by answering their questions about how to adapt to their new environment?

Chapter 4
What is Nakedness?

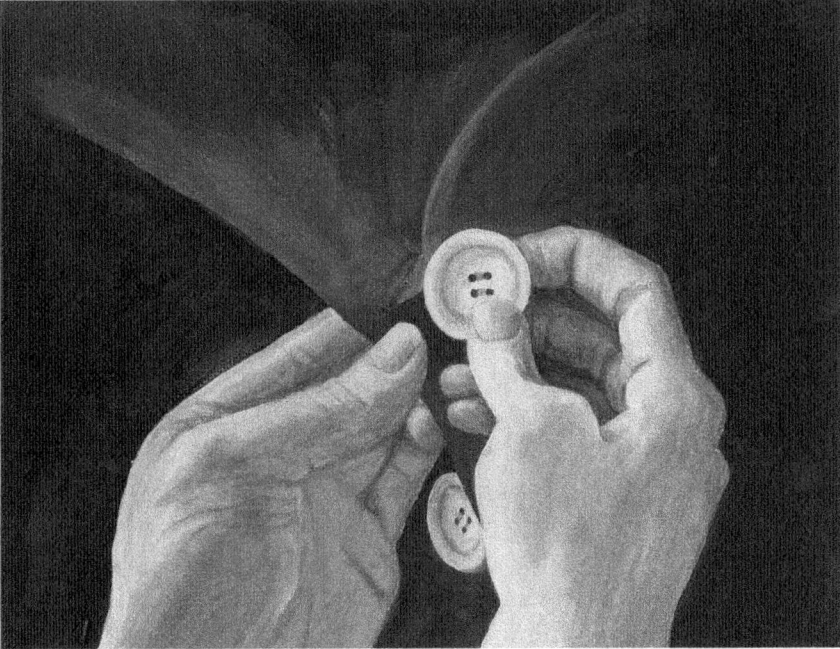

Altruism involves paying attention to what other people need, feeling empathy, and then kindly serving those needs. In this chapter the focus is on how we become aware of other people's nakedness at two levels: their physical need for protective clothing and their spiritual longing for protective truths and hope. Nakedness is explored through stories, examples of international organizations, a psychological theory, psychological and neurological research, and a theological explanation according to Swedenborg.

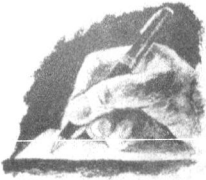

My story

Our family has a home in the mountains and it tends to get rather cold up there at the higher elevations. A few times a year we have retreats and family reunions. Over the years it has become clear to us that people who come here do not really believe us when we encourage them to bring snow-suits in January, mittens in April, and even wool sweaters in July. So we have gone to many thrift shops and stocked up on extra clothing in many sizes. As soon as I see our friends or relatives shivering, we bring out the boxes of extra clothing and let them dig for something to keep them warm. Up in the mountains, we don't care too much about fashion statements so outfits may not match, but these wool hats and down vests sure keep everyone warm.

International Altruism: Clothing the naked

There are many organizations involved in the distribution of clothing to people who need it. One altruistic group focuses particularly on shoes. They state: "Our Mission: Soles4Souls is a global not-for-profit institution dedicated to fighting the devastating impact and perpetuation of poverty. The organization advances its anti-poverty mission by collecting new and used shoes and clothes from individuals, schools, faith-based institutions, civic organizations and corporate partners, then distributing those shoes and clothes both via direct donations to people in need and by provisioning qualified micro-enterprise programs designed to create jobs in poor and disadvantaged communities" (Soles4Souls, 2014). Inspired by compassion for people who need adequate clothing, the leaders of Soles4Shoes coordinate an elaborate system of delivering resources to where they are needed the most.(See the Appendix for more information about organizations that help to provide clothing to those who need it).

Inspirational stories: Clothing the naked

In the *Holy Bible*, there is an interesting story about covering up a person who needs clothing. Although there are several scriptural stories about Noah, the most well known story is when Noah was guided by God to build a huge boat (ark) to save his family and pairs of animals during a flood. But a less well-known story happened after the flood drained away and Noah's family settled down and grew a farm. Years later, the vines on the farm were harvested for grapes and the family made some wine. In this story, Noah was lying down in his tent, coping with the effects of too much wine. His clothing fell off of him and he lay there naked. Noah's three sons became aware of this embarrassment and two of them walked into the tent backwards and respectfully draped clothing across their father to cover his naked body (*Holy Bible*, Genesis 9:21).

Psychological theory about altruism: Sorokin

Sorokin was the social psychologist mentioned in earlier chapters who studied many examples of altruism and eventually simplified his findings into a descriptive theory of five dimensions of altruism. In previous chapters, the reader can find discussions about purity, extensivity and duration. Another one of Sorokin's five dimensions is called intensity (Sorokin 1954, p.15). Sorokin suggests that altruistic individuals consider the intensity of their interest in the opportunity to serve. In general, this dimension focuses on how emotionally engaged altruistic people are when helping with a problem, such as providing affordable clothes to people who need them. For example, across the United States and Canada there are thousands of centers where altruistic people can donate their discarded clothing. Salvation Army staff and volunteers then clean and organize the clothes to sell at low prices to people who need the items. (See http://satruck.org/). This system effectively addresses the problem of people needing clothes by arranging for donations, but there is no way to know the private intensity of emotions involved in these altruistic donations.

In another example, Sew Much Comfort is a nonprofit which arranges for seamstresses to assist wounded veterans who need clothing adapted to their bodies after injuries. "Sew Much Comfort is the only organization providing FREE adaptive clothing to wounded service members. Since our founding in November 2004, we have distributed more than 134,536 pieces of adaptive clothing to our wounded" (http://www.sewmuchcomfort.org/). It is likely that the seamstresses who work face to face with each wounded warrior will be more intensely moved by this altruistic experience, compared to others who impersonally drop off their rejected clothing at the local thrift shop box. However, other people's emotions may be very private. The intensity of the kindness of donors is not always known publicly.

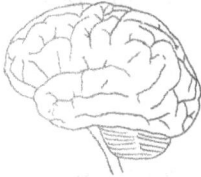

Psychological research about nakedness/clothing and altruism

When people have their basic needs met, they are in a better position to get mentally healthy. But if they are living in cold conditions without adequate coats and other protective clothing, they suffer. In the normal human brain, the hypothalamus and the brain stem are the structures that regulate the body's temperature. If a person is without adequate clothing this can lead to hypothermia, which is "when the core body temperature drops below 35 degrees C/95 degrees F. Uncontrolled, intense shivering, slurred speech, pain and discomfort occur. At core temperatures below 31 degrees C/87.8 degrees F, the pupils dilate, behavior resembles drunkenness, and consciousness is gradually lost" (Freberg, 2010, p. 260). Being naked or without adequate clothing can be very dangerous when it is extremely cold. So the question is do other people, who are warm and clothed, care about their cold neighbors? The following studies address the psychological aspects of donating clothes to make people warm. On a different level, one study addresses the psychological issues of shame due to inadequate clothing.

Some psychologists focus on the various motivations of people who donate old clothing to organizations, so that the items may be sold at reasonable prices to people who may need them. Ha-Brookshire and Hodges conducted an in-depth analysis of "consumer disposal behavior in a used clothing setting" (Ha-Brookshire & Hodges, 2009, p. 179). Most participants in this study were primarily concerned with creating space in their own closets for new items. Yet some indicated that they felt twinges of guilt about just throwing out clothing into the trash, when it could go to a thrift shop to be recycled. Sadly, very few participants even mentioned the desire to help low income people purchase this discarded clothing at low cost.

Other psychologists have narrowed their research focus onto

the long-term effectiveness of thrift shops and government agencies providing free clothing to infants of drug-abusing mothers. McCann and his colleagues (2010) investigated whether families should be reunited after this harmful exposure of drugs to vulnerable infants. In Rhode Island, research on the child welfare system showed that providing inexpensive infant clothing and other "services that address basic family needs were related to positive child welfare outcomes. The provision of basic services, such as health care and financial assistance through entitlement benefits and tangible donations, may help to establish a foundation so mothers can concentrate on recovery and parenting skills" (McCann et al, 2010, Article 19). Donors may be wary about giving clothing to children of addicts, but this research indicates that when people have enough clothing and other essentials, they are in a better position to get mentally strong. This concept is supported by the theory of the Hierarchy of Needs, explained by Abraham Maslow (Newman & Newman, 2012, p. 434).

Yet, people wear clothing not just for protection from harsh weather conditions. Clothing is also used to cover nakedness and to avoid feelings of shame and vulnerability. According to Yorke, a psychoanalytic therapist, "shame is described as a powerful and painful affect that may reach overwhelming proportions, obliterating all other feelings and thoughts. Shame carried with it a strong sense of exposure, of bodily or psychological nakedness" (Yorke, 1990, p. 14). Developmentally, most people first acquire a normal sense of shame about nakedness during their toddler or preschool years (Newman & Newman, 2012, p. 197). Later in life, people may have traumatic dreams about being caught naked in public. School-aged children also develop a "Theory of Mind" that gives them the capacity to imagine what life might be like for another person. This expands their perspective beyond their own point of view. Therefore, in normal human development, children understand their own shame due to inadequate clothing and they can vicariously understand what cold and shame might feel like for other people. As adults, they can choose to pay attention to this awareness, and make an effort to provide clothing to people who need it.

Theological perspective about spiritual naked-ness/clothing and altruism

According to Swedenborg, nakedness at a spiritual level "means one who acknowledges that there is nothing of good or truth in himself" (Swedenborg, AC 4958). One Swedenborgian scholar, named Rev. Erik Buss, asserted that some people "do not know how to be good and may not even want to learn how to be good" (Buss, 2013). He also indicated that if we are trying to be altruistic to spiritually naked people, that it is not wise to focus on those people's errors or attack them where they are vulnerable. It would be better to appeal to the spiritually naked people's ability to elevate themselves and fix their own situations. "They who are in charity scarcely see the evil of another" (Swedenborg, AC 1079). It is more helpful to offer opportunities for spiritually naked people to become aware of their own shame for a time, as this may lead to a longing for truth, as a form of spiritual, protective garments. This can help them find hope, when they are overcome with the despair that they have nothing of goodness or truth within themselves. Buss suggests that the most effective type of altruism is merciful and respectful when dealing with the spiritually naked.

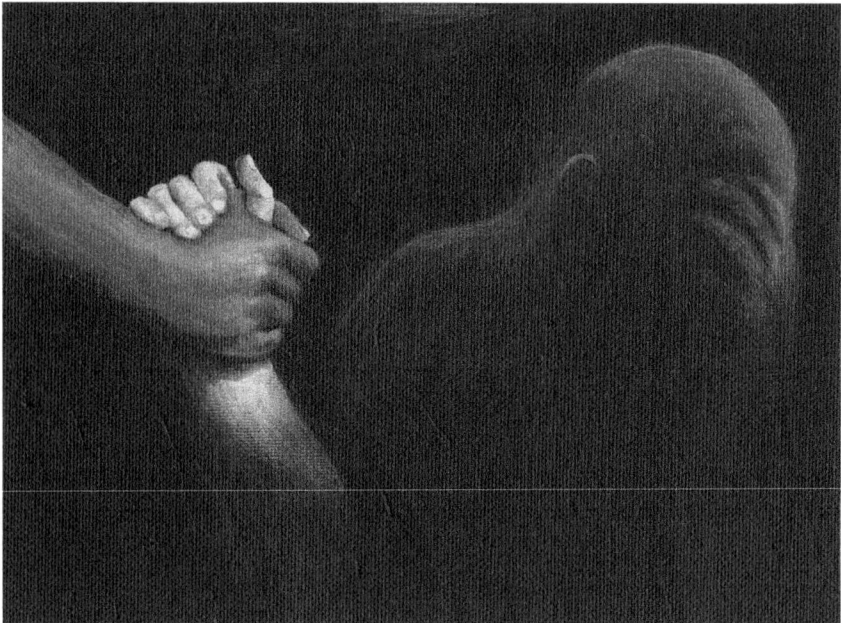

My story

Many years ago I had the opportunity to learn how vulnerable people can feel when they are spiritually naked and without hope. When I was in college, I volunteered at a crisis center answering the phones. Adolescents would call when they felt desperate and lonely. We volunteers did our best to actively listen to their stories and reflect their feelings. Our trainers told us to never belittle the feelings of hopeless adolescents, but to treat them with respect and empathy. It was pretty intense listening to their disappointments in life, and we attempted to make a genuine, human connection. I will never know if we kept them alive once they hung up the phone, but we did our best to be present during their dark moments.

More recently, in another part of the world, there was a unique solution provided to assist people who feel hopeless. A startling statistic was published that indicated that South Korea has one of the highest suicide rates for people under 40, compared to the rates in other modern countries. The leaders of the government of Seoul City decided that one thing they could do was to let desperate people know that they are not alone. So they took a bold action and redesigned a major bridge where too many suicides had occurred. "To try to counteract the number of deaths from the bridge, the Seoul City government didn't build a high fence or suicide barrier; instead it teamed with Samsung Life Insurance to take a different path, adding interactive handrails that speak directly to passersby. The handrails use motion sensors to sense people's movements and then light up with short inspirational messages crafted with the help of psychologists and suicide prevention specialists" (Starr, 2013). If this solution saves even one life, giving that person on the bridge some hope, it was worth building it.

Inspirational stories: Clothing the spiritually naked who need hope

The novel, *The Brothers Karamasov* (1880) was written by Dostoevsky, but inspired by Swedenborg's works about the afterlife. This story portrays spiritual nakedness in the form of a character with a desperate loss of hope. The plot involves following the spiritual struggles of four brothers in Russia over a century ago. Father Zosima is a spiritual advisor and he has a significant influence on at least one of the brothers. He offers hope when one of the brothers has completely lost faith in God. Father Zosima teaches this congregation that there is an afterlife and that one can actually choose a pathway to heaven or hell. He is a wonderful role model for how we can offer hope to the spiritually naked people in our lives.

Another famous author was also inspired by Swedenborg's writings. His name is Alfred Lord Tennyson. He wrote a poem in the 19th century, about discovering hope when he was grieving for the loss of a dear friend. Eventually, after years of sorrow, he looked up to God for recovery from his lingering bereavement. It is called *In Memorium, A.H.H.* He writes,

In Memorium, A.H.H.
I stretch lame hands of faith, and grope,
And gather dust and chaff, and call
To what I feel is Lord of all,
And faintly trust the larger hope
(Tennyson, 1896; Bradley, 1901).

Both Tennyson and Dostoevsky illustrated the use of bringing a spiritual dimension to recovery from despair. People who are spiritually naked are vulnerable to harsh, hellish influences, and they need protective truths. Hope can be restored when people look to God in their darkest moments, because He provides those protective truths.

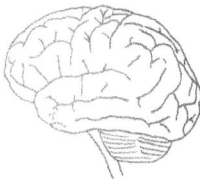

Psychological research about spiritual nakedness/clothing and altruism

Psychologists have been involved for decades in the prevention, intervention and treatment of people who feel hopeless about their future (Seligman, 1998; Snyder, 1994; Snyder & Lopez, 2002). Therapists may not call it spiritual nakedness, but they do investigate this subject carefully from a psychological viewpoint, because there is a serious vulnerability in moments of despair. For example, Praetorius & Machtmes (2005) were interested in the motivation of volunteers who answer phones at a crisis hotline. These researchers interviewed volunteers who donate their time to listen to people who have lost hope. The volunteers indicated that they were spiritually motivated to help others and to gain a deeper understanding of the human condition.

Piferi, Jobe and Jones (2006) analyzed helping behaviors and motivations following the September 11 attacks on the USA. Most often people donated money, blood and prayers. There were several motivations reported to the research team, immediately after the attack. But the motivation that was still reported even a year later was the desire to relive other people's distress.

Weil summarized research about hopeful attitudes among college students. One group of psychologists "surveyed more than 500 college students on measures of hope, depression and anxiety, then repeated the survey months later. They found students who expressed higher hope at the beginning of the study had lower measures of depression and anxiety one and two months later" (Weil, 2013, p. 42). In another study involving college students over a three-year period of time, it was found that hope was a better predictor of academic success "than intelligence, personality or previous academic achievement" (Weil, 2013, p. 43). People with high hopes usually have goals that they are pursuing, yet they are practical enough to have back-up plans. However, if students are spiritually naked, they may show this by expressing despair that they are not good enough to even live. They do not have these goals so they need counselors or advisors to help them find a reason to live and do well in college.

Strobel and her colleagues (2013) conducted research on over 800 employed adults. The researchers set up a training program in the workplace in which they emphasized a focus on the future. Then they assessed the behaviors of the people involved, and found that this future-focus program enhanced people's altruistic behaviors in the workplace. Thinking about the future includes an element of hope, not only for oneself, but also for others.

Huffmeijer and colleagues (2012) investigated the brain activity of young women who had just watched a video about a hopeless child who needed financial support. Since everyone has moments of approaching or withdrawing from new situations, these researchers decided to see if they could find out which parts of the brain are active when a person is considering whether to approach a new opportunity: such as the chance to assist a person in need. They found that when there is greater left frontal lobe neural activity, that this corresponds to the moment when a person is likely to willingly approach a new situation, and in this case to make large financial donations. However, they also found that when these young women had low activity in their left frontal lobes that they were not as willing to approach this new opportunity and donate. But that if these women were sprayed with a hormone called oxytocin into their noses, just at that time, that this made them feel warm and generous. This physiological experience had an effect on them deciding about whether to donate or not. The frontal lobe manages logical decision making, but the presence of oxytocin in one's system makes a person feel very kind and compassionate, which can affect altruistic behavior. Helping other people is not always the logical thing to do, but compassion may motivate a person to help a hopeless human being.

These few psychological studies offer explanations about the thinking, feeling and motivation of altruistic people, when they are interacting with others who feel hopeless, or spiritually naked and in need of protective truths. Volunteers are often very motivated to help and to relieve the distress of others. But offering hope is not as simple as just being optimistic and cheerful. It involves facilitating others to think about the future, to help them form realistic plans, and to assist in the formation of back-ups plans in case of disappointment. It appears that altruism is not just a logical process, as shown in the assessments of activity in the frontal lobe of the brain of kind people. More often, oxytocin (either sprayed into the nostrils or naturally released into the blood) is also present in the minds of altruistic people, while they experience generous empathy for others who are feeling hopeless.

Combining the theological, neurological and psychological perspectives helps us more fully understand the special relationship between a person who is spiritually naked and an effective altruistic helper. The spiritually naked person thinks there is nothing good or true in his/her life, and this seems to lead to moods of despair and hopelessness. The helper may be motivated to reach out and offer suggestions for how to make positive goals for the immediate future in school or work. But even more important, the helper would be wise to mention that all goodness and truth actually come from the Lord, and people can choose to bring it into their lives. This is the most protective truth of all.

Swedenborgian perspective about four levels of motivation to be altruistic

Although Sorokin was a Christian social psychologist, there is no evidence that he actually read the works of Swedenborg. However, we can integrate Sorokin's theory of altruism with Swedenborgian concepts to gain a deeper understanding. While Sorokin described intensity as one dimension of altruism, Swedenborg explains how there are many levels of that intensity. At one level we can appreciate how other people are striving to obey civil rules and laws. At a higher level, we might love other people more intensely when we see them be moral to their neighbors and family. And we can love them with an even higher intensity when we witness them serving the Lord (Swedenborg *Charity* 55-60).

In a similar vein, our intensity of compassion may increase as we discern that someone is spiritually naked at a civil, moral or spiritual level (Swedenborg HH 512, 468, 484; TCR 444). As Rev. Erik Buss indicated, a spiritually naked person has made some mistakes that we are witnessing (Buss, personal communication, 2013). They may be feeling regret and hopeless. At a civil level, the mistakes are about breaking governmental laws. At a moral level, the mistakes are regarding the way people treat each other with unfairness or malice. And at the highest level, the mistakes are about disrespect to God. When we are witnessing these mistakes in others, we would do well to simply acknowledge these errors but not dwell on them. Rather, we can serve our neighbors better by first offering intense kindness and compassion. "Genuine love involves compassionately responding to the suffering of others as if towards our own" (Klein, 1998, p. 29; Swedenborg, AC 351).

"Swedenborg distinguishes natural compassion from genuine charity, indicating that genuine charity requires looking with discernment to the quality of each neighbor. In Swedenborg's view, each person is the neighbor according to the quality of that person's good. ...When acting in charity, good love blends compassion with justice and discernment, and takes different forms depending on the different needs of each neighbor. Each neighbor is recognized equally, but a different treatment may be directed toward each neighbor's good" (Klein, 1998, p. 82; see also Swedenborg TCR 406- 419, 428, AC 1419, 6703-6712, 6812-6824; *Charity* 72-89; HH 268.)

Swedenborg tells us that there are four levels of charity, from simple helpfulness to more complex discernment (AC 3688). It takes more mental effort and focus to discern what others really need at the more sophisticated levels. Here is a paraphrased summary of the four levels of the motives of a helpful person, first with examples of clothing the naked literally, and then with examples of helping people who are spiritually naked (Swedenborg AC 3688: 3-5).

FOUR LEVELS OF CHARITY	EXAMPLES OF CLOTHING THE NAKED
Level 1) Simply give to others from the heart, so as to get a reward in heaven.	A person offers clothing to someone and hopes for a heavenly reward.
Level 2) Gives to anyone who is in distress, with no distinction about whether the receivers will use the contributions for good or ill.	A person offers clothing to people but may be shocked if a recipient uses it for evil purposes.
Level 3) Gives only to people that are thought to be upright (but may stereotype people).	A person only gives clothing to those people judged to be good, overall.
Level 4) Searches for what is good in anyone and supports that component; sees the Lord within a person and is altruistic to that part. If this is done with a full heart and with acknowledgement that all goodness comes from the Lord, this person is regenerate.	A person searches for positive aspects of people, and offers clothing with no thought of reward.

FOUR LEVELS OF CHARITY	EXAMPLES OF SPIRITUALLY CLOTHING THE NAKED BY GIVING HOPE TO THOSE IN DESPAIR
Level 1) Simply give to others from the heart, so as to get a reward in heaven.	A person offers hope to anyone, and hopes for a heavenly reward.
Level 2) Gives to anyone who is in distress, with no distinction about whether the receivers will use the contributions for good or ill.	A person offers hope to spiritually naked people but may be shocked if a recipient uses it for evil purposes.
Level 3) Gives only to people that are thought to be upright (but may stereotype people).	A person only offers hope to those groups of people judged to be good, overall.
Level 4) Searches for what is good in anyone and supports that component; sees the Lord within a person and is altruistic to that part. If this is done with a full heart and with acknowledgement that all goodness comes from the Lord, this person is regenerate.	A person searches for positive aspects of people, and offers them hope with no thought of reward.

In the next chapter, the fifth way to kindly serve the neighbor is examined: visiting the sick, both literally and spiritually.

Reflecting on your community service experiences:
1) Sorokin described five dimensions of altruism, and one of them is intensity. How intense are your feelings about doing this community service work compared to other altruistic activities you have done, such as service trips?
2) Have you noticed how you have adapted to this community service experience?
3) Are you ever bored during this experience?
4) Are you ever overwhelmed by this work feeling like there is just too much to do, and not enough workers?
5) Does this community service work involve providing clothing for people who need it, literally?
6) Does this community service work involve helping people who feel hopeless?

Chapter 5
What is Sickness?

Altruism involves paying attention to what other people need, feeling empathy, and then kindly serving those needs. In this chapter the focus is on how we become aware of other people's sickness at two levels: their need to be visited when they are physically sick, and their need for compassion when they are spiritually ill (overwhelmed with intense negative emotions). Sickness is explored through stories, examples of international organizations, a psychological theory, psychological and neurological research, and a theological explanation according to Swedenborg.

My story

Parents who care about the health of their children may develop empathy based on their own experiences and memories, or by imagining what it is like to be sick. Our two daughters tended to have severe asthma attacks during their younger years. We noticed that very cold air, spring pollen, or stress could all be triggers to bring on the terrible feeling of not being able to breathe. I have never had difficulty breathing myself, so I cannot say that I can pull on my own memory to get a feeling of empathy. But watching our toddlers struggle and wheeze was frightening, so I strived to put myself in their shoes and imagine what it was like not to be able to breathe well!

My husband had years of asthma problems a half a century ago, but it is under control now with medications. He remembers his own personal struggles with this illness, and immediately shows compassion for anyone who has trouble with their lungs. Either by recalling similar experiences from memory, or just by trying to imagine what it is like to be so sick, parents urgently seek ways to relieve their children's symptoms when illness strikes.

International Altruism: Visiting the sick

Many people are surprised to discover that it was the Islamic people of the Middle Ages that actually invented hospitals. According to the American National Institute of Heath (NIH, 2014), hospitals were first established in the Islamic countries of Iraq and Egypt. In contrast to the Europeans who had lost the ancient Greek wisdom about healing, the Islamic doctors carefully studied the works of Hippocrates, the ancient Greek physician.

After consulting the Greek medical ideas and their own theological doctrines in the Koran, the Islamic doctors created bimaristans, meaning places for ill people. These elaborate centers of healing were remarkable in that they provided services to anyone regardless of their wealth, gender, religion or ethnicity. In the bimaristan, patients would find a continuous supply of fresh water, separate sections for the mentally ill, and wards for recovery from injuries. The doctors performed surgeries and assumed that illnesses had a physical cause, rather than thinking that patients were possessed by demons. Visitors to these first hospitals in the 9th and 10th centuries were amazed at the kindness and concern shown for the ill by all of the medical staff. The Islamic religion directed members to care for their ill friends and family, and the wealthiest people altruistically provided the land and resources so the bimaristans could function effectively.

During cultural exchanges of the 11th and 12th centuries, Europeans were inspired to follow the lead of these Islamic healers and so hospitals began to be established in Spain, England and France, and eventually in the American colony of Virginia, during the next 600 years. (See the Appendix for more information).

Inspirational story: Visiting the sick

Most Americans know the true story about Helen Keller, who became seriously sick when she was a toddler in Alabama, in the 1880's. It might have been scarlet fever or meningitis, but the medical records are not clear. She was struck with permanent deafness and blindness, probably as a result of her high fever. Although she recovered from the fever, she could not communicate anymore, so no one in the family knew what to do about teaching her. Then when Helen was about six years old, Anne Sullivan was hired as a tutor. She came to visit Helen and decided to stay long enough to teach her how to communicate through her hands using sign language. This made a huge impact on the rest of Helen's life, and Anne Sullivan had become known as the "Miracle Worker" (Silverman, 1994).

Eventually, Anne Sullivan decided to be Helen's lifelong guide, helping her navigate schools and her career as a political activist, author and lecturer. Without the devoted assistance of Anne Sullivan, Helen Keller might have lived a lonely life in her permanent darkness and silence. Instead, Anne Sullivan visited Helen Keller and helped her thrive in spite of the limitations of her illness. (Later in life, Helen Keller wrote a book called *My Religion* (Keller, 1927), based on her studies of the theological works of Swedenborg. This book was later re-written for a broader audience by Rev. Dr. Ray Silverman, entitled *Light in my Darkness* (Silverman, 1994)).

Psychological theory about altruism: Sorokin

Sorokin was the social psychologist who studied many examples of altruism and eventually simplified his findings into a descriptive theory. He asserted that there are five dimensions of altruism and in earlier chapters the reader will find descriptions of purity, duration, intensity, and extensivity. The fifth dimension is called adequacy (Sorokin 1954, p.15), which means to "implement love effectively in the world...pursue learning objectives that are deemed necessary to serve others well" (Post, 2003, p. 154).

In the case of visiting sick people, Sorokin suggested that altruistic individuals ought to consider the adequacy of their skills. When visitors come to see patients who are dying in a hospice facility, the visitors need to know what to say and how to act. So many people feel awkward in this situation and think, "I have no idea what to say!" They could learn adequate communication skills from Hospice Chaplains. According to research done by health care scholars, "Chaplains are specialists in offering spiritual care, respecting patients' personal beliefs, whether these are specifically religious or more general (agnostic, atheist, humanistic). They can offer time to patients and families at this critical time and also offer support to staff. In addition, they can help patients from different faith traditions" (Pugh, Smith & Salter, 2010). When visitors come to the bedside of very sick patients, Chaplains suggest that it is best to offer comforting words and an opportunity to listen to the patient's views about dying. Medical staff may not have the time to do this as they are assigned the responsibility of managing many patients' physical needs. Chaplains indicate that visitors to hospitals will be more adequate and effective if they bring a calm, non-anxious presence, rather than a hurried mood of anxiety. Further, they could even be guided by hospice specialists on how to adequately make patients comfortable in their dying days.

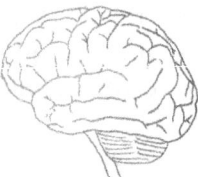

Psychological research about sickness and altruism

Psychologists try to describe, explain and predict human behavior. They often do this by first observing people and then forming theories that explain the patterns. Then the theories need to be tested to see if they are valid. The following studies involve analyses of the mental functioning and behavior of people who are actively engaged in empathy and altruistic behavior. Some of them are particularly focused on caring for sick people.

Nearly half a century ago, a psychologist named Batson created a concept called the Empathy-Altruism Theory. Batson asserted that it is necessary to first feel some empathy for others, before engaging in an altruistic response. Since then, he and his colleagues have conducted numerous studies to assess the validity of the assumption that "prosocial motivation associated with feeling empathy for a person in need is directed toward the ultimate goal of benefiting that person, not toward some subtle form of self-benefit" (Batson et al, 1988, p. 52).

Burks, Youll and Durschi (2012) investigated Batson's theory that empathy is a necessary condition for the motivation to be altruistic, especially when interacting with sick people and wanting to improve their welfare. They used over 100 subjects in a study involving several questionnaires about social desirability, empathy and altruism. They found a positive, significant correlation between empathy and altruism. However, "no significant associations were found between social desirability and altruism or between social desirability and empathy" (Burks, Youll & Durschi, 2012, p. 395). This means that it is not enough to just do what is socially expected, such as sending a card to a sick person. It is important to focus on developing true empathy for sick people, as this emotional state of mind may lead to a genuine motivation to do some altruistic behaviors, such as visiting hospitals and assisting in making sick people comfortable.

In a different study, Batson and his colleague studied an interesting variable that affects altruism. They referred back to the famous Biblical story of the Good Samaritan who helped a sick stranger (*Holy Bible* Luke 10). In this study, the experimental participants were 47 theological seminary students at Princeton University. Some of these students in the study had been individually asked to go give a talk about the Good Samaritan in a nearby building, while the others were individually asked to go to a nearby building and give a talk on some neutral subject. In each group, the other variable was how much the participants were told to hurry: some were told to rush over there, and others were not given this sense of hurry.

In every individual subjects' experience, it was planned that an actor would be encountered along the pathway to that other building, and the actor pretended to be in such pain that he was slumped over and apparently quite sick. Then each individual theological school student was unobtrusively observed to see if he/she stopped along the path. Only 40% of them stopped to assist the apparently sick person, and it did not seem to make a difference if the participant was prompted by the psychologists to think about the story of the Good Samaritan. What mattered was whether the participant was in a hurry. "Those in less of a hurry stopped to offer help more" (Darley & Batson, 1973, p. 100). So even if people are committed to becoming ordained clergy and inclined to have empathy, if they are in a hurry they are less likely to be altruistic to a sick person.

Lamm, Batson and Decety (2007) also investigated aspects of Batson's Empathy-Altruism Theory as it applied to situations where there were well people trying to take the perspective of sick people. In this research, fMRI images were taken of the brains of well subjects while they watched videos of patients who were in pain after medical treatments. The subjects were told to either 1) imagine the feelings of the patient, or 2) imagine oneself in the patient's situation. Then some subjects were informed that the medical treatment had been either 1) successful, or 2) not successful.

They found the following results. Lamm writes, "Behavioral measures demonstrated that perspective-taking and treatment effectiveness instructions affected participants' affective responses to the observed pain. Hemodynamic changes were detected in the insular cortices, anterior medial cingulate cortex (aMCC) amygdala, and in visual areas including the fusiform gyrus. Graded responses related to the perspective-taking instructions were observed in middle insula, aMCC, medial and lateral premotor areas, and selectively in left and right parietal cortices. Treatment effectiveness resulted in signal changes in the perigenual anterior cingulate cortex, in the ventromedial orbitofrontal cortex, in the right lateral middle frontal gyrus, and in the cerebellum. These findings support the view that humans' responses to the pain of others can be modulated by cognitive and motivational processes, which influence whether observing a conspecific (fellow human being) in need of help will result in empathic concern, an important instigator for helping behavior" (Lamm, Batson, & Decety, 2007, p. 42). Therefore, neuroscientists have identified some of the most active parts of the brain involved during the process of perspective-taking and empathy. Batson claimed that this is evidence supporting the assertion that empathy is necessary before actually doing something altruistic, such as visiting a sick person.

Simon-Thomas and other research scientists (2012) also studied the neural activity in the brains of people when they were prompted to feel compassion. For contrast, they made a distinction between these two types of feelings: "compassion, an emotion that orients people toward vulnerable others and prompts caregiving, and pride, a self-focused emotion that signals individual strength and heightened status" (Simon-Thomas et al, 2012, p. 635). They did fMRI images of 55 people while they were watching pictures that might induce pride or compassion or just neutral experiences. The subjects also told the researchers what feeling they were experiencing, at the same time that brain scans were conducted.

While subjects felt compassion and perception of other people's pain, there was neural activity in the midbrain periaqueductal gray area and the right inferior frontal gyrus. In contrast, when subjects felt pride, the posterior medial cortex was active. This region is already known to be active when people are thinking about themselves, rather than other people. During moments of pride there was also a reduction in activity in the right inferior frontal gyrus and the anterior insula. Therefore, when a person feels pride it may be difficult to simultaneously feel compassion and concern for other people who are sick. One could generalize from these findings that when a person is visiting a sick friend, it is best to set aside any feelings of being proud of oneself for being so noble, and focus instead on the ill person who is suffering.

In summary, based on these recent studies about altruistic attitudes and behaviors, it appears that sincere empathy for a sick person may be the precursor of kind behaviors towards the ill. However, this may be interrupted if the altruistic person is in a hurry or is consumed with self-pride. The evidence from these psychological studies indicates that concentrating on the perspective of a person in a sickbed in an unhurried and unselfish manner may lead to more genuine empathy, compassion and altruistic actions.

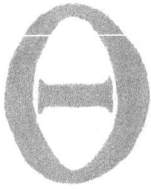

Theological perspective about spiritual sickness and altruism

According to Swedenborg's Writings which offer an internal sense to the story in Matthew 25, the spiritually sick person is "one who acknowledges that he is in evil" (Swedenborg, AC 4958); and "the sick are those who are distressed by evils and falsities and are to be visited, by some who bring comfort and by others who bring a remedy " (Swedenborg, D.Min 4586). However, according to the Swedenborgian scholar Rev. Erik Buss, sickness cannot be cured through intellectual discussions, but by going to the Lord and repenting (personal communication, 2013). Therefore, one short visit to chat with a spiritually sick person about spiritual health may not be enough. It is unrealistic to assume that spiritual illness will be cured by a visitor, quickly. This may be a long process, and it may take extra effort and patience on the part of the visiting friend.

What is spiritual sickness? It could take many forms, but

most stem from either an overwhelming love of self or worldly possessions. For example, greed can be taken to the extreme so that it becomes the main focus of a person's life. Greed and extreme accumulation of wealth can become an obsession filling a person's mind, replacing any previous concern about family and friends. It is a spiritual sickness as it destroys the person's healthy love for people in the intense pursuit of gaining more money or property. If this sick person acknowledges that he/she is obsessed with this evil love of possessions, that is the first step towards health. It takes great patience and skill to visit a spiritually sick person, so very often they are just avoided and judged from a distance.

We are told that visitors ought to bring an attitude of kindness, just as the Good Samaritan brought oil to soothe the sick man's wounds. Then we are to offer truth, symbolized by the Good Samaritan pouring wine for the beaten man. Finally, we are to offer instruction, represented by the Good Samaritan bringing the man to an inn (*Holy Bible* Mark 6:13, Luke 10: 25-37, Swedenborg AE 375:42). Initial kindness nourishes the spiritually sick person with a sphere of mercy. However, when the time is right, the spiritually sick person needs to acknowledge that other people have been harmed by the obsession that is out of control, whether it is greed, pornography, hatred, jealousy, addiction or deception. This acknowledgement might be the turning point towards spiritual health, if the person is willing to learn something true and apply it to life.

Over 50 years ago, some compulsive gamblers felt their lives had become unmanageable, so they decided to form a support group for recovering addicts based on Alcoholics Anonymous. They adapted the well-known 12 steps of recovery to the case of compulsive gambling:

"1. We admitted we were powerless over gambling - that our lives had become unmanageable.

2. Came to believe that a Power greater than ourselves could restore us to a normal way of thinking and living.

3. Made a decision to turn our will and our lives over to the care of this Power of our own understanding.

4. Made a searching and fearless moral and financial inventory of ourselves.

5. Admitted to ourselves and to another human being the exact nature of our wrongs.

6. Were entirely ready to have these defects of character removed.

7. Humbly asked God (of our understanding) to remove our shortcomings.

8. Made a list of all persons we had harmed and became willing to make amends to them all.

9. Make direct amends to such people wherever possible, except when to do so would injure them or others.

10. Continued to take personal inventory and when we were wrong, promptly admitted it.

11. Sought through prayer and meditation to improve our conscious contact with God as we understood Him, praying only for knowledge of His will for us and the power to carry that out.

12. Having made an effort to practice these principles in all our affairs, we tried to carry this message to other compulsive gamblers.

The 12 Step Program is fundamentally based on ancient spiritual principles and rooted in sound medical therapy. The best recommendation for the program is the fact that it works" (Gamblers Anonymous, 2014).

The sponsor at a 12 Step meeting is like the Good Samaritan, first offering kindness as he/she sits near the participants with an attitude of mercy and compassion. But eventually the sponsor nudges them to make such an inventory and to think about the truth that good relationships matter more than their greed for money. The next step is for the participants to go make amends with all the people they have harmed in their overzealous pursuit of wealth for their own benefit. This reparation of relationships is what Swedenborg calls a conjunction of goodness and truth, and it is in this process that the Lord can help people gain insights and heal their spiritual sickness of greed (Swedenborg, AE 815).

My story

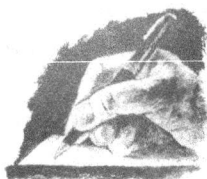

Recently I ran into a man I have known since childhood. We ate lunch in a cafe and got caught up, starting with what we had in common. We both enjoy motorcycling and reading.

We are also both challenged by raising our strong-willed daughters to adulthood. We laughed and cried a bit over shared memories and disappointments in life. But soon it became apparent that this man was absolutely baffled by his two failed marriages. He had acquired a gorgeous home, lots of vehicles, enough money to go on fancy vacations, but the women in his life kept leaving him. He could not figure it out. He shared, "Sure I gambled and am a work-aholic, but how else was I going to be able to pay the mortgage and buy those expensive gifts my family and current girlfriend expected from me?" After a while I asked him what would happen if he simplified his life and lived with fewer possessions? Would this give him more time to develop different kinds of relationships? He's still sick with anger at the women in his life and blames them for his unhappiness.

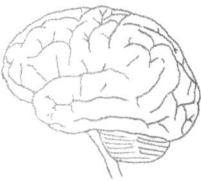

Psychological research about spiritual sickness and altruism

William James lived over a century ago in a Swedenborgian family in Boston, and he was the first American psychologist and a prolific author. James is known for integrating many Swedenborgian spiritual principles into his secular, psychological books. In William James' book, *Varieties of Religious Experiences* (1902), he discussed people who are sick in their souls. He stated that the sick soul finds that "unsuspectedly from the bottom of every fountain of pleasure…, something bitter rises up: a touch of nausea, a falling dead of the delight, a whiff of melancholy…." that brings "a feeling of coming from a deeper region and often have an appalling convincingness" (James, 1902, p. 136). But James also believed in the ability for individuals to transform themselves, spiritually, and overcome their spiritual sicknesses.

Bill Wilson lived in New York in the 1930's and he struggled with a serious alcohol addiction and could not find anyone to help him recover. He read both Swedenborg's Writings about spiritual growth and the *Varieties of Religious Experiences* (James, 1902). These works helped him formulate a method called the 12 steps of recovery. This led to the founding of Alcoholics Anonymous. The 12 step method of spiritual recovery from the sickness of addiction has helped millions of people, as they support each other. The concepts of recovery did not require affiliation with any particular organized church, but they were centered on faith to God and charity to the neighbor. The 12 steps spell out a way to allow God to heal from unhealthy relationships with alcohol, gambling, narcotics, sex, or overeating.

But the program also allows people who are sick with addiction to help others who are addicted. In fact it is in the twelfth step that altruism happens. For example, "...carry this message to other compulsive gamblers" (Gamblers Anonymous, 2014). Hence, the line between the altruistic helper and the helped person blurs. Part of the effective recovery of an individual addict involves helping other addicts recover, too.

In addition to analyzing social behaviors during recovery, psychologists also search for neural correlates to altruistic attitudes and memories. When one sick person says to another sick person, "I know how you feel because I suffer from the same thing", this engages the parts of the brain dedicated to memory and empathy.

In an effort to map the brain structures according to the functions performed in each region, four neuro-scientists named Beadle, Tranel, Cohen and Duff (2013) have done research about which parts of the brain are involved when a person shows empathy for other people who are sick or in distress. Based on previous research, they reported that it is well established that the following brain structures seem to be active during empathy: "ventromedial prefrontal cortex, amygdala, anterior insula, cingulate" (2013, Article 69). However, these scholars also discovered another brain structure that is involved when people experience empathy. They did this through a process of comparing people with brain damage in their memory areas to those with no brain damage. They found that the hippocampus is an additional brain structure involved in empathy. This means that if a subject is not able to recall and declare what is remembered, it makes it very difficult to experience genuine empathy. But for people with normal brains, it is helpful to draw on their own memories of life experiences when assisting the needy. These memories can help empathy and kindness grow.

Swedenborgian perspective about four levels of motivation to be altruistic

Sorokin suggested that adequacy is an important dimension of altruism, however, he did not provide much detail. In Swedenborg's writings, we are told that we can choose to make the effort to be adequate in our useful endeavors in four aspects of life, arranged on a continuum, and these efforts will lead to genuine happiness.

Bodily needs
Material needs
Social needs
Spiritual needs

At the most basic level, we can choose to serve others' bodily needs such as making them physically comfortable during times of illness. Being adequate at this level means learning from medical professionals about how to move a bedridden patient, or when to administer certain pain medications to a person in hospice. At the next level, Swedenborg tells us that we can strive to serve others according to their material needs. For example, when dealing with sick family members we can make sure to provide adequate facilities with in-home care or at a hospital. This might involve paying for the right kind of bed and other equipment. Then at the next level, Swedenborg instructs that we can serve others according to their social needs. So this might mean adequately arranging for family and friends to come to the bedside of the ailing patient, and guiding them on what to say to be most effective during critical moments. Finally, Swedenborg states that the highest level of useful service involves one's relationship with God. If we are helping our sick friends, and treating them as if they are each Jesus himself, then we will experience a deep happiness. We can also provide for the spiritual needs of the patient by arranging visits and rituals involving clergy (Swedenborg CL 18).

"Swedenborg distinguishes natural compassion from genuine charity, indicating that genuine charity requires looking with discernment to the quality of each neighbor. In Swedenborg's view, each person is the neighbor according to the quality of that person's good. ...When acting in charity, good love blends compassion with justice and discernment, and takes different forms depending on the different needs of each neighbor. Each neighbor is recognized equally, but a different treatment may be directed toward each neighbor's good" (Klein, 1998, p. 82; see also Swedenborg TCR 406-419, 428, AC 1419, 6703-6712, 6812-6824; *Charity* 72-89; HH 268).

As in previous chapters, the altruistic attitudes and behaviors of the following four levels of charity can be illustrated with examples of literally visiting sick people and attending to spiritually sick people, according to one's motivations (Swedenborg AC 3688: 3-5).

"We can think of uses as the ways in which individuals serve others and the community, and the ways in which others and the community serve the individual" (Klein, 1998, p. 34).

FOUR LEVELS OF CHARITY	EXAMPLES OF VISITING THE SICK
Level 1) Simply give to others from the heart, so as to get a reward in heaven.	A person visits any sick person and hopes for heavenly rewards.
Level 2) Gives to anyone who is in distress, with no distinction about whether the receivers will use the contributions for good or ill.	A person visits sick people but may be shocked if a recipient uses it for evil purposes.
Level 3) Gives only to people that are thought to be upright (but may stereotype people).	A person only visits those groups of sick people judged to be good, overall.
Level 4) Searches for what is good in anyone and supports that component; sees the Lord within a person and is altruistic to that part. If this is done with a full heart and with acknowledgement that all goodness comes from the Lord, this person is regenerate.	A person searches for positive aspects of people, and visits the sick with no thought of reward.

FOUR LEVELS OF CHARITY	EXAMPLES OF SPIRITUALLY VISITING THE SICK BY HELPING THEM HEAL FROM NEGATIVE EMOTIONS
Level 1) Simply give to others from the heart, so as to get a reward in heaven.	A person visits any spiritually sick person, and hopes for a heavenly reward.
Level 2) Gives to anyone who is in distress, with no distinction about whether the receivers will use the contributions for good or ill.	A person visits spiritually sick people but may be shocked if a recipient uses it for evil purposes.
Level 3) Gives only to people that are thought to be upright (but may stereotype people).	A person only visits spiritually sick people who are judged to be good, overall.
Level 4) Searches for what is good in anyone and supports that component; sees the Lord within a person and is altruistic to that part. If this is done with a full heart and with acknowledgement that all goodness comes from the Lord, this person is regenerate.	A person searches for positive aspects of people, and visits spiritually sick people with no thought of reward.

In the final chapter, our attention is turned to the sixth way to be kind to others: visiting people who are in prison, literally or spiritually.

Reflecting on your community service experiences:
1) Sorokin described five dimensions of altruism, and one of them is adequacy of skills. Do you see other workers in this organization who are very skilled and effective in what they do to help people?
2) Have you noticed any improvements in your own skills since you started doing community service here? Are these physical skills, cognitive skills or social-emotional skills?
3) Is this setting for your community service work focused on helping physically sick people? How do you feel about this?
4) Is this setting for your community service work focused on helping spiritually/emotionally sick people? How do you feel about this?
5) Have you had an experience in which you worked with other staff or volunteers collaboratively to solve a problem?
6) Do you admire the positive attitude of anyone you have met in this setting?

Chapter 6
What is Imprisonment?

Altruism involves paying attention to what other people need, feeling empathy, and then kindly serving those needs. In this chapter the focus is on how we become aware of other people's imprisonment at two levels: their need to be visited when they are literally imprisoned, and their need for therapy when they are spiritually imprisoned (trapped in false ideas). Imprisonment is explored through stories, examples of international organizations, a psychological theory, psychological and neurological research, and a theological explanation according to Swedenborg.

My story

In the 1980's, I was given the opportunity to become a college professor inside a maximum-security prison. Previously, I had taught psychology courses in various colleges, but it had never occurred to me to actually go behind bars and teach the same concepts to people who were in prison for rape and murder. I seriously wondered if they would want to learn about human behavior! After months of preparation and training, I cautiously started working there and stayed for five years because I loved it.

I taught hundreds of inmates in courses such as Introductory Psychology, Social Psychology and Adolescent Psychology. I tried to see them as regular students, who happen to all be in the same color uniforms. I did not ask them about their crimes or even dwell on why they were in prison. But I did ask them to learn the ideas about human behavior and apply them as they rebuilt their lives. Most of the time, the inmate students appreciated the respectful attention that all prison faculty members showed them (in contrast to how most guards treated inmates). I know I benefitted from my interactions with these students, who just happened to be in prison. Gradually I saw them less as a group of prisoners, and more as individual people, each with unique life stories.

The more I paid attention to them as individuals, the more I was able to perceive their life stories and then notice how they each felt about imprisonment and freedom. Most longed for the day when the prison doors would open and they would be physically released into the free world. But what was especially fascinating was hearing them share about how they were working to free themselves from more abstract types of imprisonment. For example, some were enrolled in a Quaker program about alternatives to violence, and they were learning that they could break away from the false idea that all conflicts must be handled with brutal aggression. These former murderers were acquiring assertive verbal skills to handle social difficulties, and with it they were experiencing spiritual freedom.

International Altruism: Visiting the imprisoned

In a small town in western Pennsylvania, there is a church group devoted to visiting imprisoned people. They are a social outreach department affiliated with Mt. Saint Peter Parish. The staff and volunteers seek justice rather than revenge as they approach inmates with an attitude of forgiveness. They strive to follow in the footsteps of Jesus who taught us to love our enemies. The altruistic people in this church group offer these suggestions to anyone who is visiting someone in prison around the globe:

"Pray for those who are imprisoned and for those forced to live in unjust situations.

Pray for the inmates' families, because they are suffering too.

Encourage crime victims and victims of domestic violence to seek pastoral or secular professional counseling.

Guard against racism; practice inclusion, not exclusion.

Learn more about the plight of those unjustly imprisoned for political and religious beliefs, as well as how to advocate for their release.

Be mindful that we are all members of the human race and equal in God's eyes" (Mt. Saint Peter Parish, 2014. See the Appendix for more information).

Inspirational stories: Visiting the imprisoned

One of my former colleagues wrote a fictional novel about imprisonment in the context of true historical events. Dr. Sylvia M. Shaw combined her love of both Mexican history and spiritual ideals into her book entitled *Paradise Misplaced* (2012). Shaw is a Swedenborgian scholar who intentionally wove themes about freedom into her novel.

There is a Mexican character in Shaw's novel named Benjamin, who is physically locked up against his will. While in prison for an extended time period, he decides to contemplate and write about his life. His wife, Isabel, has a profound influence on him as he ponders the purpose of his existence. She gently nudges him to think twice about his selfishness, which is crippling his happiness. The way she talks to Benjamin when she regularly visits him in the Mexican prison leads to his transformation to a more spiritually aware human being than he had been before his incarceration. He bravely deals with both his physical imprisonment and spiritual imprisonment as the story unfolds.

Psychological theory about altruism: Sorokin

In five previous chapters, Sorokin's theory of altruism was described in terms of five dimensions. But who was Sorokin? He was raised in Russia during the revolution, and then immigrated to the USA to work as a social-psychologist at Harvard University. He even established the world's first Research Center for Creative Altruism. He writes, "in 1918, I was hunted from pillar to post by the Russian Communist Government. At last I was imprisoned and condemned to death. Daily, during six weeks, I expected to be shot, and witnessed the shooting death of my friends and fellow prisoners. During the subsequent four years of my stay in Communist Russia I underwent other painful experiences and observed, to the heartbreaking point, endless horrors of human bestiality, death and destruction. Exactly in these conditions I jotted down in my diary the following observations.... Whatever may happen in the future, I know that I have learned three things which will remain forever convictions of my heart as well as my mind. Life, even the hardest life, is the most beautiful, wonderful, and miraculous treasure in the world. Fulfillment of duty is another marvelous thing making life happy. This is my second conviction. And the third is that cruelty, hatred, violence, and injustice never can and never will be able to create a mental, moral, or material millennium. The only way toward it is the royal road of all-giving creative love, not only preached but consistently practiced" (Sorokin, 1954, p. xi).

In reaction to his personal experiences with the horrors of war and imprisonment, Sorokin decided to emphasize the positive aspects of humanity, such as altruism. He had been imprisoned several times during the Russian Revolution and became an astute observer and recorder of these events. As a political prisoner he spent time listening to the sorrows of his fellow inmates. Although he witnessed brutality from the guards, he also noticed that imprisoned people could be kind to each other.

These intense experiences helped Sorokin formulate his theory of altruism decades later as a professor in the USA. He asserted that any positive, altruistic act could be described in terms of five dimensions: duration, extensivity, intensity, purity and adequacy. Duration refers to the length of time doing helpful behaviors. Extensivity refers to helping family members as well as people from far away places and cultures. Intensity is an indication of the extent of emotional engagement of an altruistic person when being helpful. Purity is the most private aspect of altruism, because it refers to the sincerity of the motives of the altruistic individual. Finally, adequacy is the dimension of altruism that refers to the skilled effectiveness of any helpful behavior. Sometimes this means the helper should be professionally trained, but other times, this might just mean avoiding unhelpful words and knowing the right thing to say during a tragedy (Post, 2003; Post, Johnson, McCullough, & Schloss, 2003).

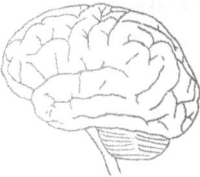

Psychological research about altruism: visiting the imprisoned

Many psychologists are interested in imprisonment, looking at both the inmates and the visitors. Among the following summaries of research are results about investigations focused on empathy, communication, adjustment, forgiveness, and sensitivity to the pain of others. By closely examining several aspects to this highly charged experience of visiting imprisoned people, psychologists can offer some impartial conclusions to help us understand its importance.

On the subject of visiting the imprisoned, Sheri Oz, who is a psychologist giving advice to readers on the internet site called Demand Media, writes, "one of the most important things prison inmates require of their friends and family is help maintaining personal dignity. One way to do that is by being honest at all times. Your honesty keeps communication open and clear, and stands in contrast to all the humiliating experiences your friend may face in prison. That means that if you are hurt or ashamed by having a friend in jail, for example, be honest about it. Honesty gives your statements credibility, so when you say 'I care about you' your friend will know that you mean that too. According to a report published by the Minnesota Department of Corrections, almost 40 percent of prison inmates never receive visitors; that same study found that visits by friends and families can help reduce the chances of recidivism. When you do visit, understand that your friend may not be feeling sociable on some visiting days and it will be a comfort to him or her if you are tolerant and compassionate in spite of that" (Oz, 2014).

The concepts of altruism arrived at by Sorokin correlate well with what Oz writes. Both would advocate that when motivated to visit the imprisoned, it is wise to be purely honest, be intensely compassionate, prepare adequate/helpful words to say, and keep on visiting for the duration of the imprisonment. Most people are more likely to just visit friends and family, but some will even extend their altruism to visit total strangers.

Casey-Acevedo and Bakken (2002) focused their research on the effects of visitors occasionally coming to women's prisons. They analyzed the number of visits that hundreds of imprisoned women experienced, and the resulting social adjustment of the female inmates. Almost two thirds of the women who were mothers did not have visits with their children. The study found that over 75% of the prison visitors who did come were not family, but adult friends. Unfortunately, this long-term separation from family seems to cause more difficulty in prison adjustment, making matters worse. The researchers speculate that if more family members were to visit inmates that this might help with the psychological and social adjustment of the prisoners. The research team wondered if family members would continue to avoid visiting their imprisoned relatives if they knew how very much it could help the prisoner, psychologically.

Krueger and other researchers (2013) were interested in the degree of empathy that people feel when someone has been sent to prison. Can people feel empathy for both the imprisoned person and the victim of violent crimes? Previous neuroscientists have identified that the moment when oxytocin (a neurotransmitter) is present in the bloodstream that subjects report feeling kind and compassionate. Normally the brain releases oxytocin at certain times, but it can also be administered in a nasal spray to have a short-term effect. Krueger and others found that in a controlled study with healthy men as subjects, that right after this nasal injection of oxytocin, the subjects showed an increase in their compassion for victims of crime. In addition, the subjects were less likely to wish that they could punish offenders of criminal offenses. The researchers wondered about the extent of compassion for the criminals, and suggested that this be studied further.

Farrow and other neuroscientists (2001) were also curious about how people look at criminals: do they have empathy and a longing to forgive imprisoned criminals? Instead of examining the effects of the neurotransmitter oxytocin, the researchers in this study examined the neural activity in brains of ten adults to identify which structures of the brain may be active during these states of mind. Just when these ten adults were saying that they felt empathy for criminals, the following parts of their brains were active: the frontal lobe especially in some of the left portions, and the temporal lobe particularly in the anterior middle portion. In contrast, when the subjects felt like forgiving the criminals, their posterior cingulate cortex was active, which is a part of the brain that has often been associated with wondering about the future.

Vanderlaan, Bauer and vanOyen Witvliet (2000 and 2001) have also been doing a series of research studies on whether people can forgive criminal offenders. They found that when the subjects of their study spent time contemplating an attitude of unforgiveness, in the sense of feeling hurt or holding a grudge against criminals, that they were also more aroused, negative and actually less in control at that moment. In contrast, when these same people in the study imagined forgiveness of criminals, they experienced feelings of empathy and sensed that they were more positive, less aroused and more in control at that exact time. In another study by Vanderlaan and colleagues, actual victims of crimes were asked to imagine that they purposely thought about forgiving criminals. In those moments, they also felt more empathy and a positive desire for reconciliation. However, the stronger the grudge and desire for vengeance reported by these victims, the more negative they felt during the study.

Guo and other neuroscientists (2013) investigated a different aspect of crime. They examined the effects of people watching so much violence that it leads to desensitization, or the numbing of feelings about how horrific violence can be. They used fMRI imaging and verbal reports to measure this process. They found that right after watching very violent videos, that people indicated that they had much less empathy for the pain of other people who were victims of crime, and there was much less activity in the insula and anterior cingulate cortex. These two regions of the brain are usually quite active when people show concern for other people and a desire to be altruistically involved in making them feel better. This could be generalized to mean that observers of violent crimes may temporarily lose their sensitivity for the victims involved if they are so used to watching violence on films or in real life. If these desensitized observers visit inmates, they might have lost their compassion for the victims of the crimes involved, which could be detrimental to everyone involved.

In summary, many psychologists and neuroscientists have been investigating various aspects of the situation involved in people visiting criminals in jail. More visits seem to help inmates adjust, but the attitude of the visitors matters a great deal. It is complicated because family members need to be honest about the shame involved in having a relative behind bars, and yet they also need to be forgiving. Visitors who have seen an excessive amount of violence in their lives might lose their sensitivity to the pain that victims feel and forget to keep them in mind during their visits to the prisoner who conducted violent crimes.

So, according to the research studies reported here, it can be concluded that it is important for prison visitors to strive to imagine what imprisonment is like, to communicate honestly, to try to forgive the inmate, and to maintain empathy for both victims and inmates. This is actually quite challenging and apparently very few people do it well.

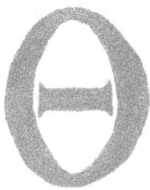

Theological perspective about spiritual imprisonment and altruism

According to Swedenborg who offers an internal sense for the story in Matthew 25 about the six ways to serve the neighbor, "he that is 'in prison,' is one who acknowledges that he is in falsity" (Swedenborg, AC 4954-4959). Spiritual imprisonment can happen anywhere that a person is living a life that is built on a lie or false assumption. The person feels trapped in this falsity and may be uncertain how to become free of this entanglement.

For example, there are some people who have intrusive

thoughts that make them feel very uneasy. People with this condition called OCD (Obsessive-Compulsive Disorder) are trapped in repeated thought patterns that lead to tremendous anxiety. These obsessive thoughts crowd out other concepts in the mind and may lead the person to do compulsive behaviors in order to reduce the anxiety. Compulsive behaviors include excessive washing of hands and countertops to rid the environment of germs. The person with OCD may feel stuck in the false assumption that if only the physical environment is extremely clean that then he will feel safe. If the person acknowledges that this makes no sense, then maybe he can begin to get therapeutic help to reduce these obsessions and compulsions that are dominating his life (About OCD, 2104; American Psychiatric Association, 2013).

My story

Recently at a college graduation party, I learned about some people who seemed trapped in a social custom. I had the chance to finally meet the parents of my psychology students. While the majority of the time everyone at the party was jovial and excited about college graduation, at one point I was invited into a private conversation with one parent. My student explained that he needed to translate because his mother did not speak English, only Spanish. She wanted to talk to me because she was very curious about my books about the psychology of women.

Over the next half hour, with careful translations back and forth, we communicated about the plight of many women that she knows in Central America. She explained that she volunteers to visit some of the uneducated women who are victims of male machismo, which means intense masculine pride. Unfortunately, this cultural attitude often leads to violence and repression against women. The majority of the women in her home country experience rape, physical abuse or denial of an education simply because of their gender. The social custom of male machismo is to treat women as second-class citizens and give them few choices. In our conversation, we agonized over how hard it is for most men in her culture to change, as they are trapped in this false assumption that women have no worth. So actually, we concluded that both the men and women in that machismo culture seem spiritually imprisoned.

Inspirational story: Visiting the spiritually imprisoned

C.S. Lewis was a reader of Christian books and Swedenborg's writings. Based on these ideas he created many inspired stories and suggestions to a broad audience, in his own unique manner. On the subject of people's perception of being spiritually imprisoned, Lewis writes, "If you think of this world as a place intended simply for our happiness, you find it quite intolerable: think of it as a place of training and correction and it's not so bad. Imagine a set of people all living in the same building. Half of them think it is a hotel, the other half think it is a prison. Those who think it a hotel might regard it as quite intolerable, and those who thought it was a prison might decide that it was really surprisingly comfortable. So that what seems the ugly doctrine is one that comforts and strengthens you in the end…the people who hold a pretty stern view of it become optimistic" (Lewis, 1992, p.103-104). Lewis is referring to how people may feel restrained by false ideas about doctrine, until they realize that God gave us truths such as the 10 Commandments to make us happy and free.

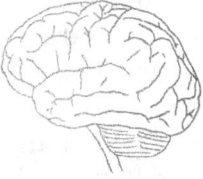

Psychological research about spiritual imprisonment and altruism

From a psychological perspective, people who feel trapped are often diagnosed with OCD, which is Obsessive-Compulsive Disorder. Their mental patterns get overly focused on certain negative thoughts and they feel compelled to repeat certain behaviors over and over. Eventually, if untreated, these patients spend way too many hours per day locked in these obsessive thoughts and behavioral rituals. They feel psychologically imprisoned and become desperate to change their lives. It is extremely difficult for them to change on their own, so they go to therapists. Clinical therapists depend on the research of neuroscientists to understand the physiology of OCD and treatment effectiveness.

One group of neuroscientists, led by Hoexter (2013) examined 43 OCD patients and various treatments for their condition. They measured the amount of gray matter in the frontal lobes of their brains, before and after they received treatments. Those OCD patients that had less volume in their frontal lobes responded better to drug treatments for three months (fluoxetine). In contrast, those patients with OCD that had much more volume of gray matter in their frontal lobes before the intervention responded better to talking treatments for three months. More gray matter in the frontal lobe usually indicates that a person is more intelligent and better able to make careful decisions. However, in the case of a person with OCD, the thinking that is done in the frontal lobe is out of control and the person is trapped in those repetitive, anxious thoughts and unnecessary behavior patterns.

The talking treatment employed here was Cognitive-Behavior Therapy, or CBT (Beck, 2013), which "is a type of psychotherapeutic treatment that helps patients understand the thoughts and feelings that influence behaviors. CBT is commonly used to treat a wide range of disorders including... anxiety. CBT is generally short-term and focused on helping clients deal with a very specific problem. During the course of treatment, people learn how to identify and change destructive or disturbing thought patterns that have a negative influence on behavior" (Cherry, 2014).

In a similar experiment, Huyser and his colleagues (2013) also investigated the physiological changes in the brains of OCD patients, but they focused on 29 adolescents rather than adults. They also examined how the brain can actually change in the volume of gray matter of the frontal lobe after treatments involving Cognitive-Behavioral Therapy. In addition to changes in the physical brain, the patients' thinking patterns changed and their compulsive behaviors were reduced. This is very encouraging news indicating that people who are trapped in their false ideas about how to be safe can actually be taught by therapists about how to change the way they think and behave. Their brains actually change in the process and they can start to feel free.

Similarly to a person with OCD who is stuck on false thoughts about imagined germs, it could be just as frightening to be stuck thinking about spiritual trangressions. For instance, imagine a person who feels trapped in the false idea that God has abandoned him because of promiscuous sexual behavior done during adolescence. Before reaching adulthood, adolescents might experiment sexually (which is not ideal), but the truth is that the Lord is very forgiving. What matters is whether this adult with a fully developed rational mind justifies those earlier sexual indiscretions or asks the Lord for forgiveness. If this adult makes a sincere commitment before the Lord to be faithful in marriage, and then lives up to this promise of fidelity, there is no need to be obsessed with thoughts of eternal punishment (see Swedenborg *Conjugial Love*). However, it may take the professional skills of a trained Cognitive-Behavioral Therapist to help this patient change his thought patterns so that he can feel free and really loved by the Lord.

A therapist is like a skilled visitor to a spiritual prison, someone who is altruistically helping patients point out any false ideas, so that they can change the way they think, behave, and feel. Then this will help people feel true freedom.

Swedenborgian perspective about four levels of motivation to be altruistic

Psychologists can choose to be secular or spiritual in their therapeutic approach to helping people who are literally in prison or spiritually trapped in false ideas. Even though therapists are not supposed to be proselytizing a specific religion, they can increase their effectiveness in helping others when they carefully consider their own spiritual motives. They can also choose to use wise discernment as they carefully diagnose and treat their patients. In this manner, their efforts to help even the most difficult inmate or OCD patient can be spiritually inspired and full of true compassion. Klein writes, "Swedenborg's vision of a life of charity emphasizes a person's daily work or employment, and also a person's ongoing connections or relationships with others. Swedenborg defines charity as doing what is good and right in every work, office, employment, and activity in our lives with others" (Klein, 1998, p. 35; see also Swedenborg AC 8121, 8122, TCR 422, 423).

"Swedenborg distinguishes natural compassion from genuine charity, indicating that genuine charity requires looking with discernment to the quality of each neighbor. In Swedenborg's view, each person is the neighbor according to the quality of that person's good. ...When acting in charity, good love blends compassion with justice and discernment, and takes different forms depending on the different needs of each neighbor. Each neighbor is recognized equally, but a different treatment may be directed toward each neighbor's good" (Klein, 1998, p. 82; see also Swedenborg TCR 406-419, 428, AC 1419, 6703-6712, 6812-6824; *Charity* 72-89; HH 268).

Swedenborg tells us that there are four levels of charity, from simple helpfulness to more complex discernment (AC 3688). It takes more mental effort and focus to discern what others really need at the more sophisticated levels. Here is a paraphrased summary of the four levels of the motives of a helpful person, first with examples of visiting the imprisoned person literally, and then with examples of visiting the imprisoned person spiritually.

FOUR LEVELS OF CHARITY	EXAMPLES OF VISITING PRISONERS
Level 1) Simply give to others from the heart, so as to get a reward in heaven.	A person visits anyone who is in prison and hopes for heavenly rewards.
Level 2) Gives to anyone who is in distress, with no distinction about whether the receivers will use the contributions for good or ill.	A person visits prisoners but may be shocked if a recipient uses it for evil purposes.
Level 3) Gives only to people that are thought to be upright (but may stereotype people).	A person only visits those groups of people in prison judged to be good, overall.
Level 4) Searches for what is good in anyone and supports that component; sees the Lord within a person and is altruistic to that part. If this is done with a full heart and with acknowledgement that all goodness comes from the Lord, this person is regenerate.	A person searches for positive aspects of people, and visits prisoners with no thought of reward.

FOUR LEVELS OF CHARITY	EXAMPLES OF SPIRITUALLY VISITING PRISONERS BY HELPING THEM ADJUST THEIR FALSE IDEAS
Level 1) Simply give to others from the heart, so as to get a reward in heaven.	A person helps any people change their thinking, and hopes for a heavenly reward.
Level 2) Gives to anyone who is in distress, with no distinction about whether the receivers will use the contributions for good or ill.	A person helps people change their thinking but may be shocked if a recipient uses it for evil purposes.
Level 3) Gives only to people that are thought to be upright (but may stereotype people).	A person only offers help with changing thinking patterns to those groups of people judged to be good, overall.
Level 4) Searches for what is good in anyone and supports that component; sees the Lord within a person and is altruistic to that part. If this is done with a full heart and with acknowledgement that all goodness comes from the Lord, this person is regenerate.	A person searches for positive aspects of people, and offers help with changing thinking patterns with no thought of reward.

In the following section, there is a conclusion about these six ways to be kind to others, both literally and spiritually.

Reflecting on your community service experiences:
1) Sorokin had literally been imprisoned during his adolescence and saw a very dark side of humanity. Yet he chose to look for ways that human beings flourish with kindness. During your community service work have you ever seen very negative behavior or attitudes? How do you react to this?
2) When you look at the community service work you are doing, what is the real need that you are addressing: literally or spiritually?
3) Do you wish the government or churches did more to help people with these needs?
4) If you ran an organization like this, what would you do differently?
5) Why do you think God permits people to have such serious problems?
6) Have you ever literally visited people in a prison?
7) Have you ever talked to people who seem seriously trapped in some false idea that really limits their lives? Have you ever met anyone with OCD?
8) What do you think about using CBT to help people change their thinking patterns?

Conclusion

Altruism is one of the finest aspects of human beings. While we are not the only species to kindly take care of our young, we seem to be the only living creatures that can decide to be helpful for spiritual reasons. In other words, we can make a conscious choice to spend time, energy, money or other resources for others, and do it because it is a way to give back to God. We can hear each other's amazing stories, and read inspiring novels. We can read the New Testament and abide by the words of Jesus as He guides us to serve others in six ways. We can learn from the Biblical interpretations of Swedenborg that these six ways also have an internal sense for how we can be kind to other people at a deeper level. Then, once we understand, we are in a position to deliberately and purposefully apply these ideas to life.

In this book, we analyzed altruism through many lenses and multiple examples:

Personal stories
Novels with interesting characters
International organizations
Psychological theories
Psychological and neurological research
Theological doctrines

These examples and ideas inspire us to devote some of our time on this planet as altruistic people. Research gives us clues about the parts of our brains that are involved during thoughts, feelings and acts of kindness. Theories provide explanations of psychological patterns of altruism. Memorable stories from personal life and novels provide us with role models to emulate. Organizations with lofty missions stir our imagination to show how people can solve global problems on a grand scale. And theological concepts help us make meaning of it all: theology shows us why we would do well to be kind to others.

True altruism is an attitude that can infuse our home life, our hobbies, our paid employment and our volunteer activities. Any duty can be elevated with an attitude of altruism. Swedenborg calls this being useful to others, not just ourselves. He asserts that it is not enough for us to become smart and to feel positively towards others; we will be more complete once we actually get out there and do acts of kindness, as well.

So, in closing, let's think about some examples of young adults who have decided to steer their careers towards altruistic endeavors. As a college professor, I have enjoyed coaching adolescents as they become adults and make career plans, and so I have plenty of examples:

Recently, one young woman finished college and 8 years of business experience and decided to go back to school to earn an MBA, with a concentration in Social Entrepreneurship. This will enable her to work with corporate leaders to direct some of their profits to altruistic organizations that help feed and clothe people in need.

Just today, another young woman told me that she has decided to apply to graduate school to learn how to manage non-profit organizations such as schools.

One young man is in the process of becoming a psychology major, and dreams of one day helping abused children who have lost hope. His unselfish interest in this population has lasted for a long duration, and he hopes to make it his life work once he develops adequate skills.

Several young people have volunteered for the Peace Corps, reaching out extensively to people on the other side of the globe who need better access to clean water and enough food.

One former student of mine is now a lawyer who focuses his expertise on helping estranged immigrants navigate the legal system of America.

Another former student studied education and then decided to become a foster parent to children of diverse races, and her facebook narrative indicates how intensely she is involved in this work.

Several students have gone on to get theological training and now inspire their congregations with the purity of their articulated motivations to do community service projects.

One of the former inmate students I taught inside the prison is now released and working as an addiction counselor to people who are suffering from that illness.

So, what will you do with this one life that God has given to you? How will you give back, and in the process experience joy flowing from God through you and out to the people in your world? Maybe it will be in your paid employment, or perhaps in your volunteer efforts, or maybe right in your own home with your family. You get to choose from all the many kinds of kindnesses.

Appendix A
Abstracts of psychological and neurological studies

Chapter 1:

Perspectives of volunteers in emergency feeding programs on hunger, its causes, and solutions.
doi: 10.1016/S1499-4046(06)60074-2
By Edlefsen, Miriam S.; Olson, Christine M.
Journal of Nutrition Education and Behavior, Vol 34(2), Mar-Apr 2002, 93-99.
Examines the social beliefs of volunteers in emergency feeding programs (EFPs) regarding hunger and whether volunteer experiences broadened understanding of hunger. An interpretivist paradigm and qualitative methods were used. 17 volunteers (aged 50-77 yrs) were recruited and interviewed from three EFPs. Interviews were analyzed using the constant comparative method. Volunteering in EFPs increased volunteers' awareness of the prevalence of hunger in their communities. More involved volunteers had a greater understanding of the life situations of the hungry. The volunteers felt that increasing self-sufficiency and private responses were appropriate solutions to hunger. The volunteers' attitudes and social beliefs were similar to those of the general public.

Right supramarginal gyrus is crucial to overcome emotional egocentricity bias in social judgments.
doi: 10.1523/JNEUROSCI.1488-13.2013
By Silani, Giorgia; Lamm, Claus; Ruff, Christian C.; Singer, Tania
The Journal of Neuroscience, Vol 33(39), Sep 25 , 2013, 15466-15476.
Humans tend to use the self as a reference point to perceive the world and gain information about other people's mental states. However, applying such a self-referential projection mechanism in situations where it is inappropriate can result in egocentrically biased judgments. To assess egocentricity bias in the emotional domain (EEB), we developed a novel visuo-tactile paradigm assessing the degree to which empathic judgments are biased by one's own emotions if they are incongruent to those of the person we empathize with. A first behavioral experiment confirmed the existence of such EEB, and two independent fMRI experiments revealed that overcoming biased empathic judgments is associated with increased activation in the right supramarginal gyrus (rSMG), in a location distinct from activations in right temporoparietal junction reported in previous social cognition studies. Using temporary disruption of rSMG with repetitive transcranial mag-

netic stimulation resulted in a substantial increase of EEB, and so did reducing visuo-tactile stimulation time as shown in an additional behavioral experiment. Our findings provide converging evidence from multiple methods and experiments that rSMG is crucial for overcoming emotional egocentricity. Effective connectivity analyses suggest that this may be achieved by early perceptual regulation processes disambiguating proprioceptive first-person information (touch) from exteroceptive third-person information (vision) during incongruency between self- and other-related affective states. Our study extends previous models of social cognition. It shows that although shared neural networks may underlie emotional understanding in some situations, an additional mechanism subserved by rSMG is needed to avoid biased social judgments in other situations.

Humble persons are more helpful than less humble persons: Evidence from three studies.
doi: 10.1080/17439760.2011.626787
By LaBouff, Jordan Paul; Rowatt, Wade C.; Johnson, Megan K.; Tsang, Jo-Ann; Willerton, Grace McCullough
The Journal of Positive Psychology, Vol 7(1), Jan 2012, 16-29.
Connections between humility and other prosocial qualities led us to develop a *humility–helpfulness hypothesis*. In three studies, humble persons were more helpful than less humble persons. In Study 1, participants (n = 117) completed self-report measures of humility, the Big Five, and helpfulness. In Study 2, participants (n = 90) completed an implicit measure of humility and were presented with an unexpected opportunity to help someone in need. In Study 3, participants (n = 103) completed self-report and implicit measures of humility and were presented a similar helping opportunity. Humility and helpfulness correlated positively when personality and impression management were controlled. Humble participants helped more than did less humble participants even when agreeableness and desirable responding were statistically controlled. Further, implicit humility uniquely predicted helping behavior in an altruistic motivation condition.

Volunteering and well–being: Is pleasure–based rather than pressure–based prosocial motivation that which is related to positive effects?
doi: 10.1111/jasp.12012
By Vecina, María L.; Fernando, Chacón
Journal of Applied Social Psychology, Vol 43(4), Apr 2013, 870-878.
This article seeks to establish whether prosocial motivation in a sample of 251 volunteers is based on pleasure and not on pressure, which is related to the states of general well-being (hedonic and eudaimonic

measures) and the various states of well-being specifically associated with volunteerism (volunteer satisfaction, volunteer engagement, and study enjoyment), all of this irrespective of the age of the volunteers. An analysis of partial correlations and linear regression leads to the conclusion that volunteerism undertaken as a non-obligatory, planned helping activity, sustained over time and within an organizational context, is not always associated with positive effects in terms of well-being. It seems that these positive effects are related to pleasure-based prosocial motivation.

Response of dorsomedial prefrontal cortex predicts altruistic behavior.
doi: 10.1523/JNEUROSCI.6193-11.2012
By Waytz, Adam; Zaki, Jamil; Mitchell, Jason P.
The Journal of Neuroscience, Vol 32(22), May 30 , 2012, 7646-7650.
Human beings have an unusual proclivity for altruistic behavior, and recent commentators have suggested that these prosocial tendencies arise from our unique capacity to understand the minds of others (i.e., to mentalize). The current studies test this hypothesis by examining the relation between altruistic behavior and the reflexive engagement of a neural system reliably associated with mentalizing. Results indicated that activity in the dorsomedial prefrontal cortex — a region consistently involved in understanding others' mental states — predicts both monetary donations to others and time spent helping others. These findings address long-standing questions about the proximate source of human altruism by suggesting that prosocial behavior results, in part, from our broader tendency for social-cognitive thought.

Chapter 2:

Open source software: A community of altruists.
doi: 10.1016/j.chb.2010.04.008
By Baytiyeh, Hoda; Pfaffman, Jay
Computers in Human Behavior, Vol 26(6), Nov 2010, 1345-1354.
To learn about what drives people to devote their time and expertise to creating and supporting free/open source software, a survey with Likert-scaled items measuring different types of motivations was sent to contributors of several open source projects. Open-ended comments were used to illustrate the Likert-scaled items and open-ended questions allowed respondents to express their reasons for participating in these open source communities. Results indicate that the open source contributors (n =110, 38 paid to work on OSS projects and 72 volunteers) are motivated primarily by a sense of altruism as well as the desire to create and learn. Payment did not significantly impact the reasons for contributing to OSS projects. The comments and open-ended

questions validated the findings and indicated that building a "Utopian" community—the desire to help for the greater good world-wide—is one of the most important motivators. Also, respondents revealed that they join and persist as members of open source communities because they enjoy the freedom to create and share free software, tools and knowledge with others inside and outside the community.

Bernt, F.M. (1989) Being religious and being altruistic: A study of college service volunteers. Personality and Individual Differences, 10(6), 663-669.
245 college students surveyed; 90% were Catholic. Of these 88% applied to a service corps after college. Those who planned to do service work after college scored higher on the Quest Scale (questioning religion) and lower on the extrinsic scale of religious orientation. Intrinsic religiosity is a mature stage that most college students have not yet achieved.

Social capital and individual motivations on knowledge sharing: Participant involvement as a moderator.
doi: 10.1016/j.im.2010.11.001
By Chang, Hsin Hsin; Chuang, Shuang-Shii
Information & Management, Vol 48(1), Jan 2011, 9-18.
The Internet is a communication channel that allows individuals to share information and knowledge. However, it is not obvious why individuals share knowledge with strangers for no apparent benefit. What are the critical factors influencing such behavior? To attempt to understand this paradox, we combined the theories of social capital and individual motivation to investigate the factors influencing knowledge sharing behavior in a virtual community, applying a participant involvement concept to analyze the moderating effects of individual motivation on knowledge sharing behavior. By analyzing the results of a survey using a questionnaire, we found that altruism, identification, reciprocity, and shared language had a significant and positive effect on knowledge sharing. Reputation, social interaction, and trust had positive effects on the quality, but not the quantity, of shared knowledge. Participant involvement had a moderating effect on the relationship of altruism and the quantity of shared knowledge. Theoretical and managerial implications are discussed.

Community service and identity development in adolescence.
By Yates, Miranda
Dissertation Abstracts International: Section B: The Sciences and Engineering, Vol 56(5-B), Nov 1995, 2908.
In the 1990s, a substantial number of U.S. adolescents have participated

in community service programs. Advocates submit that service promotes prosocial development in participants. A review of the literature, however, reveals inconsistent outcomes and little theoretical discussion of processes that might result in developmental change. Drawing on Erikson's (1968) writings which stressed the social-historical component of identity, this study connects community service to a theoretical understanding of identity development in adolescence. It reports on a service program that required 160 Black parochial high school juniors to serve at a soup kitchen as part of a year-long course on social justice. Students came from middle and lower-middle class families. Data included questionnaires, group interviews, year-long observations, and soup kitchen essays written quarterly. The analysis focused on the essays which were coded for transcendent reflections and emotional and relational engagement. Adapting Luckmann's (1991) scheme, reflections were parsed into 3 ordered levels: (1) examining preconceptions about homeless people, (2) comparing one's life situation to another's, and (3) evaluating justice and responsibility. 47% of the students made reflections in the initial essay and an additional 27% included reflections in a subsequent essay. Three findings indicate a pattern of developmental change: (1) reflections in the initial essay were related to prior service experience, (2) students who made reflections in the initial essay were likely to make them in subsequent essays, and (3) reflections became more encompassing over the yeat. Sadness in earlier essays was related to reflections in subsequent essays. Feeling good about helping and learning about the life of a person served were associated with more encompassing reflections. Anger and reflectivity predicted future volunteer plans. In sum, service evoked strong emotions and encouraged reflections on homelessness.

Chapter 3:

The mentalizing network orchestrates the impact of parochial altruism on social norm enforcement.
doi: 10.1002/hbm.21298
By Baumgartner, Thomas; Götte, Lorenz; Gügler, Rahel; Fehr, Ernst
Human Brain Mapping, Vol 33(6), Jun 2012, 1452-1469.
Parochial altruism—a preference for altruistic behavior towards ingroup members and mistrust or hostility towards outgroup members—is a pervasive feature in human society and strongly shapes the enforcement of social norms. Since the uniqueness of human society critically depends on the enforcement of norms, the understanding of the neural circuitry of the impact of parochial altruism on social norm enforcement is key, but unexplored. To fill this gap, we measured brain activity with functional magnetic resonance imaging (fMRI) while sub-

jects had the opportunity to punish ingroup members and outgroup members for violating social norms. Findings revealed that subjects' strong punishment of defecting outgroup members is associated with increased activity in a functionally connected network involved in sanction-related decisions (right orbitofrontal gyrus, right lateral prefrontal cortex, right dorsal caudatus). Moreover, the stronger the connectivity in this network, the more outgroup members are punished. In contrast, the much weaker punishment of ingroup members who committed the very same norm violation is associated with increased activity and connectivity in the mentalizing-network (dorsomedial prefrontal cortex, bilateral temporo-parietal junction), as if subjects tried to understand or justify ingroup members behavior. Finally, connectivity analyses between the two networks suggest that the mentalizing-network modulates punishment by affecting the activity in the right orbitofrontal gyrus and right lateral prefrontal cortex, notably in the same areas showing enhanced activity and connectivity whenever third-parties strongly punished defecting outgroup members.

Experiential Learning Strategies for Promoting Adolescents' Voluntarism in Hong Kong.
doi: 10.1007/s10566-005-9003-6
By Cheung, Chau-kiu
Child & Youth Care Forum, Vol 35(1), Feb 2006, 57-78.
Nurturing adolescents' voluntarism--their willingness to help needy strangers-appears to hinge on the experiential learning component embedded in a volunteer training program. Evidence for this is presented from an experimental study carried out in Hong Kong. Although program participants did not differ in voluntarism from their classmates who did not participate in the program, those who devoted more time to volunteer services were ultimately significantly higher on voluntarism. Those who volunteered for services to new immigrants, to people with mental retardation, and to chronic patients had significantly higher voluntarism levels than others. Early voluntarism did not significantly affect their volunteer participation. These findings support the role of experiential learning in the adolescent's development of voluntarism.

Mentoring: A Proven Delinquency Prevention Strategy.
doi: 10.1037/e302022003-001
By Grossman, Jean Baldwin; Garry, Eileen M.
OJJDP Juvenile Justice Bulletin; Apr 1997; 7 pp [US Department of Justice (DOJ)].
Article concerning the Big Brothers/Big Sisters (BB/BS) of America, that continues to operate today as the largest mentoring organization of

its kind. BB/BS is a federation of more than 500 agencies that serve children and adolescents. Its mission is to make a difference in the lives of young people, primarily through a professionally supported one-to-one relationship with a caring adult, and to assist them in reaching their highest potential as they grow into responsible men and women by providing committed volunteers, national leadership, and standards of excellence. In this article topics discussed include the following: the Federal role in mentoring; Public/Private Ventures (P/PV) evaluation of Big Brothers/Big Sisters; Office of Juvenile Justice and Delinquency Prevention (OJJDP) and the P/PV evaluation results; and the evaluation of the Juvenile Mentoring Program (JUMP). Additional readings and futher information resources are also provided.

Empathy for the social suffering of friends and strangers recruits distinct patterns of brain activation.
doi: 10.1093/scan/nss019
By Meyer, Meghan L.; Masten, Carrie L.; Ma, Yina; Wang, Chenbo; Shi, Zhenhao; Eisenberger, Naomi I.; Han, Shihui Han
Social Cognitive and Affective Neuroscience, Vol 8(4), Apr 2013, 446-454.

Humans observe various peoples' social suffering throughout their lives, but it is unknown whether the same brain mechanisms respond to people we are close to and strangers' social suffering. To address this question, we had participant's complete functional magnetic resonance imaging (fMRI) while observing a friend and stranger experience social exclusion. Observing a friend's exclusion activated affective pain regions associated with the direct (i.e. firsthand) experience of exclusion [dorsal anterior cingulate cortex (dACC) and insula], and this activation correlated with self-reported self-other overlap with the friend. Alternatively, observing a stranger's exclusion activated regions associated with thinking about the traits, mental states and intentions of others ['mentalizing'; dorsal medial prefrontal cortex (DMPFC), precuneus, and temporal pole]. Comparing activation from observing friend's vs stranger's exclusion showed increased activation in brain regions associated with the firsthand experience of exclusion (dACC and anterior insula) and with thinking about the self [medial prefrontal cortex (MPFC)]. Finally, functional connectivity analyses demonstrated that MPFC and affective pain regions activated in concert during empathy for friends, but not strangers. These results suggest empathy for friends' social suffering relies on emotion sharing and self-processing mechanisms, whereas empathy for strangers' social suffering may rely more heavily on mentalizing systems.

Compassion, Altruism, Contemplative Practices, and Psychological Well-Being

doi: 10.1037/e602652013-001
By Rangan, Rachna K.; O'Connor, Lynn E.; Berry, Jack W.; Stiver, David J.; Choi, Kevin W.; Li, Yanlin; Ark, Winfred; Hanson, Rick
2013 [American Psychological Association (APA)].

The last decade has seen an explosion of interest in contemplative practices and their potential to promote positive psychological outcomes and general wellbeing. While contemplative practices have traditionally been rooted in religious traditions, currently there is a significant expansion of secular contemplative practice, often referred to as "mindfulness." Contemplative traditions may all share similar goals; to develop concentration, deepen understanding and insight, and to cultivate awareness of the interconnectedness of all life and compassion towards self and others. Given the findings demonstrating the benefits of contemplative practices in promoting overall well being, the need to better understand the factors that influence these outcomes has been mounting. We approached this issue by conducting an anonymous online empirical study involving practitioners from a wide range of contemplative traditions. In a study of 2413 practitioners including the Tibetan and Theravada Buddhist, Centering Prayer, Yoga and secular mindfulness traditions, we found that all groups, compared to non-practitioners, enjoyed psychological benefits. These included significantly lower rates of depression, anxiety, and empathic-distress, and higher rates of empathy, agreeableness, conscientiousness, openness and compassionate altruism towards strangers. Within the contemplative practitioners' groups we found intensity of practice significantly correlated with these positive outcomes. Comparing religion-based practices with secular or non-religious practices, we found that those practicing from a religious tradition were significantly higher on resilience as measured by general factor of personality and compassionate altruism towards strangers. Further, comparing traditions whose practice is other-focused with those whose practice is self-focused, we found that those who endorsed other-focused practice were significantly lower in depression, empathic distress, and anxiety, and significantly higher in cognitive empathy and altruism towards strangers.

Chapter 4:

Socially responsible consumer behavior? Exploring used clothing donation behavior.

doi: 10.1177/0887302X08327199
By Ha-Brookshire, Jung E.; Hodges, Nancy N.
Clothing & Textiles Research Journal, Vol 27(3), Jul 2009, 179-196.

Most research on socially responsible consumer behavior has focused on consumer purchasing behavior; therefore, little is known about it during the product disposal stage. This study seeks an in-depth understanding of consumer disposal behavior in a used clothing donation setting. An interpretive analysis revealed that the primary motivation for participants' used clothing donation behavior is the need to create space in the closet for something new. The threat of feelings of guilt played a significant role throughout the process prior to donation, specifically in the decision whether to discard or donate a clothing item. Participants experienced both utilitarian and hedonic values regarding their donation behavior, and these values in turn affected future donation intentions. A conceptual model based on the study findings that integrates a theory of reasoned action framework with a consumer values perspective is proposed. Study implications and future research avenues are also discussed.

Asymmetric frontal brain activity and parental rejection predict altruistic behavior: Moderation of oxytocin effects.

doi: 10.3758/s13415-011-0082-6
By Huffmeijer, Renske; Alink, Lenneke R. A.; Tops, Mattie; Bakermans-Kranenburg, Marian J.; van IJzendoorn, Marinus H.
Cognitive, Affective & Behavioral Neuroscience, Vol 12(2), Jun 2012, 382-392.
Asymmetric frontal brain activity has been widely implicated in reactions to emotional stimuli and is thought to reflect individual differences in approach–withdrawal motivation. Here, we investigate whether asymmetric frontal activity, as a measure of approach–withdrawal motivation, also predicts charitable donations after a charity's (emotion-eliciting) promotional video showing a child in need is viewed, in a sample of 47 young adult women. In addition, we explore possibilities for mediation and moderation, by asymmetric frontal activity, of the effects of intranasally administered oxytocin and parental love withdrawal on charitable donations. Greater relative left frontal activity was related to larger donations. In addition, we found evidence of moderation: Low levels of parental love withdrawal predicted larger donations in the oxytocin condition for participants showing greater relative right frontal activity. We suggest that when approach motivation is high (reflected in greater relative left frontal activity), individuals are generally inclined to take action upon seeing someone in need and, thus, to donate money to actively help out. Only when approach motivation is low (reflected in less relative left/greater relative right activity) do empathic concerns affected by oxytocin and experiences of love withdrawal play an important part in deciding about donations.

Services used by perinatal substance-users with child welfare involvement: A descriptive study.
doi: 10.1186/1477-7517-7-19
By McCann, Kenneth J.; Twomey, Jean E.; Caldwell, Donna; Soave, Rosemary; Fontaine, Lynne Andreozzi; Lester, Barry M.
Harm Reduction Journal, Vol 7, Aug 31 , 2010, Article 19.
Background: Substance use during pregnancy often leads to involvement in the child welfare system, resulting in multiple social service systems and service providers working with families to achieve successful child welfare outcomes. The Vulnerable Infants Program of Rhode Island (VIP-RI) is a care coordination program developed to work with perinatal substance-users to optimize opportunities for reunification and promote permanency for substance-exposed infants. This paper describes services used by VIP-RI participants and child welfare outcomes. Methods: Data collected during the first four years of VIP-RI were used to identify characteristics of program participants, services received, and child welfare outcomes: closed child welfare cases, reunification with biological mothers and identified infant permanent placements. Descriptive Results: Medical and financial services were associated with positive child welfare outcomes. Medical services included family planning, pre- and post-natal care and HIV test counseling. Financial services included assistance with obtaining entitlement benefits and receiving tangible support such as food and clothing. Conclusions: Findings from this study suggest services that address basic family needs were related to positive child welfare outcomes. The provision of basic services, such as health care and financial assistance through entitlement benefits and tangible donations, may help to establish a foundation so mothers can concentrate on recovery and parenting skills. Identification of services for perinatal substance users that are associated with more successful child welfare outcomes has implications for the child welfare system, treatment providers, courts and families.

Giving to others during national tragedy: The effects of altruistic and egoistic motivations on long-term giving.
doi: 10.1177/0265407506060185
By Piferi, Rachel L.; Jobe, Rebecca L.; Jones, Warren H.
Journal of Social and Personal Relationships, Vol 23(1), Feb 2006, 171-184.
The debate over altruistic and egoistic motivations for helping has a long history and evidence supports both motives. Immediate and sustained helping following the September 11 attacks on the United States were examined. The three most commonly reported helping behaviors were donating money, praying, and donating blood. Six reported motivations for giving emerged: to relieve one's own distress, to relieve the

other's distress, to show patriotism, to show civic responsibility, the desire for support in a similar situation, and knowing someone involved. Less giving was reported after 1 year than immediately following the event. The only motivation related to sustained giving was giving to relieve the other's distress. Results are discussed using two theories of helping.

Volunteer crisis hotline counselors: An expression of spirituality.
By Praetorius, Regina Trudy; Machtmes, Krisanna
Social Work & Christianity, Vol 32(2), 2005, 116-132.
This article addresses an often overlooked motivation for volunteers—spirituality. The authors were asked to conduct a qualitative research study of motivations and benefits of volunteering at the local crisis center's 24-hour crisis hotline. The main questions asked of study participants were, what was the initial motivation for volunteering, and what keeps them coming back. Among the findings was a spiritual aspect to these volunteers' motivation to "work the lines." This spiritual motivation took on a variety of forms, including a desire to "give back" (altruism), a new perspective of one's own life and perceived challenges and obstacles, deeper understanding of the human condition, and realizing the interconnectedness among us all as part of the social fabric. The article shares these findings more in depth using the volunteers' own words.

The future starts today, not tomorrow: How future focus promotes organizational citizenship behaviors.
doi: 10.1177/0018726712470709
By Strobel, Maria; Tumasjan, Andranik; Spörrle, Matthias; Welpe, Isabell M.
Human Relations, Vol 66(6), Jun 2013, 829-856.
Future-oriented cognition has been shown to be an important driver of several functional behaviors. In the present article, we build and test theory empirically on the influence of dispositional future focus on organizational citizenship behavior (OCB). We integrate future focus research with regulatory focus theory to examine the two regulatory foci (i.e. promotion and prevention focus) as mediating mechanisms through which future focus influences five distinct organizational citizenship behaviors (i.e. altruism, civic virtue, conscientiousness, courtesy, and sportsmanship). In line with our hypotheses, results from a study of 845 employees show that future focus has a positive influence on altruism, civic virtue, and courtesy over and above important predictors of OCB identified in previous research. Mediation analyses support our theoretical model, indicating that different OCBs are influenced by future focus through either promotion or prevention focus at work.

A psychoanalytic approach to the understanding of shame.
By Yorke, Clifford B.
Sigmund Freud House Bulletin, Vol 14(2), 1990, 14-28.
Examines the origins and effects of the emotion of shame. Shame is described as a powerful and painful affect that may reach overwhelming proportions, obliterating all other feelings and thoughts. Shame carries with it a strong sense of exposure, of bodily or psychological nakedness, linked with an external as well as an internal referent. There is always an awareness of an observer who is disapproving or condemnatory. Although shame is a normal affect, its excessive and repeated experience can border on pathology. Observations from a mother–toddler group and from a nursery school, as well as several case histories, are used to illustrate the development and effects of shame in the individual.

Chapter 5:

Five studies testing two new egoistic alternatives to the empathy-altruism hypothesis.
doi: 10.1037/0022-3514.55.1.52
By Batson, C. Daniel; Dyck, Janine L.; Brandt, J. Randall; Batson, Judy G.; Powell, Anne L.; McMaster, M. Rosalie; Griffitt, Cari
Journal of Personality and Social Psychology, Vol 55(1), Jul 1988, 52-77.
The empathy-altruism hypothesis claims that prosocial motivation associated with feeling empathy for a person in need is directed toward the ultimate goal of benefiting that person, not toward some subtle form of self-benefit. We explored two new egoistic alternatives to this hypothesis. The empathy-specific reward hypothesis proposes that the prosocial motivation associated with empathy is directed toward the goal of obtaining social or self-rewards (i.e., praise, honor, and pride). The empathy-specific punishment hypothesis proposes that this motivation is directed toward the goal of avoiding social or self-punishment (i.e., censure, guilt, and shame). Study 1 provided an initial test of the empathy-specific reward hypothesis. Studies 2 through 4 used three procedures to test the empathy-specific punishment hypothesis. In Study 5, a Stroop procedure was used to assess the role of reward-relevant, punishment-relevant, and victim-relevant cognitions in mediating the empathy-helping relationship. Results of these five studies did not support either the empathy-specific reward or the empathy-specific punishment hypothesis. Instead, results of each supported the empathy-altruism hypothesis. Evidence that empathic emotion evokes altruistic motivation continues to mount.

Empathy in hippocampal amnesia.

doi: 10.3389/fpsyg.2013.00069
By Beadle, J. N.; Tranel, D.; Cohen, N. J.; Duff, M. C.
Frontiers in Psychology, Vol 4, Mar 22 , 2013, Article 69.

Empathy is critical to the quality of our relationships with others and plays an important role in life satisfaction and well-being. The scientific investigation of empathy has focused on characterizing its cognitive and neural substrates, and has pointed to the importance of a network of brain regions involved in emotional experience and perspective taking (e.g., ventromedial prefrontal cortex, amygdala, anterior insula, cingulate). While the hippocampus has rarely been the focus of empathy research, the hallmark properties of the hippocampal declarative memory system (e.g., representational flexibility, relational binding, on-line processing capacity) make it well-suited to meet some of the crucial demands of empathy, and a careful investigation of this possibility could make a significant contribution to the neuroscientific understanding of empathy. The present study is a preliminary investigation of the role of the hippocampal declarative memory system in empathy. Participants were three patients (1 female) with focal, bilateral hippocampal (HC) damage and severe declarative memory impairments and three healthy demographically matched comparison participants. Empathy was measured as a trait through a battery of gold standard questionnaires and through on-line ratings and prosocial behavior in response to a series of empathy inductions. Patients with hippocampal amnesia reported lower cognitive and emotional trait empathy than healthy comparison participants. Unlike healthy comparison participants, in response to the empathy inductions hippocampal patients reported no increase in empathy ratings or prosocial behavior. The results provide preliminary evidence for a role for hippocampal declarative memory in empathy.

The empathy-altruism association and its relevance to health care professions.

doi: 10.2224/sbp.2012.40.3.395
By Burks, Derek J.; Youll, Lorraine K.; Durtschi, Jayson P.
Social Behavior and Personality, Vol 40(3), 2012, 395-400.

It is posited in the empathy-altruism hypothesis that altruistic motivation evoked by empathy is directed toward the ultimate goal of improving another person's welfare. In this study the empathy-altruism hypothesis was examined. Measures of altruism, empathy, and social desirability were completed by 112 individuals in a university setting. A positive and significant association was found between altruism and empathy (rs = .24, p = .01, 95% CI [.06-.41]). No significant associations were found between social desirability and altruism or between social desirability and empathy. Because the loss of capacity to feel empathy may lead to burnout, disillusionment, and reduced altruistic helping efforts, the clinical applicability and implications of these findings are particularly important to health care and other helping professions.

Darley, J.M., & Batson, C.D. (1973). From Jerusalem to Jericho: A study of situational and dispositional variables in helping behavior. Journal of Personality and Social Psychology, 27(1), 100 – 108. 47 Princeton Theological Seminary students. First personality assessments. Then told to go to another bldg to either give a talk about Good Samaritan or some neutral topic. Along the way there, each faced a person slumped over in pain. 40% of the students offered some form of help. 60% did not. Personality variables did not predict who would stop. Students had been told various levels of HURRY instructions. And those who were in the most hurry rarely stopped. Those in less of a hurry stopped to offer help more.Thinking about the story of the Good Samaritan had no effect on whether the student would stop to help.

The Neural Substrate of Human Empathy: Effects of Perspective-taking and Cognitive Appraisal.
doi: 10.1162/jocn.2007.19.1.42
By Lamm, Claus; Batson, C. Daniel; Decety, Jean
Journal of Cognitive Neuroscience, Vol 19(1), Jan 2007, 42-58.
Whether observation of distress in others leads to empathic concern and altruistic motivation, or to personal distress and egoistic motivation, seems to depend upon the capacity for self-other differentiation and cognitive appraisal. In this experiment, behavioral measures and event-related functional magnetic resonance imaging were used to investigate the effects of perspective-taking and cognitive appraisal while participants observed the facial expression of pain resulting from medical treatment. Video clips showing the faces of patients were presented either with the instruction to imagine the feelings of the patient ("imagine other") or to imagine oneself to be in the patient's situation ("imagine self"). Cognitive appraisal was manipulated by providing information that the medical treatment had or had not been successful. Behavioral measures demonstrated that perspective-taking and treatment effectiveness instructions affected participants' affective responses to the observed pain. Hemodynamic changes were detected in the insular cortices, anterior medial cingulate cortex (aMCC) amygdala, and in visual areas including the fusiform gyrus. Graded responses related to the perspective-taking instructions were observed in middle insula, aMCC, medial and lateral premotor areas, and selectively in left and right parietal cortices. Treatment effectiveness resulted in signal changes in the perigenual anterior cingulate cortex, in the ventromedi-

al orbitofrontal cortex, in the right lateral middle frontal gyrus, and in the cerebellum. These findings support the view that humans' responses to the pain of others can be modulated by cognitive and motivational processes, which influence whether observing a conspecific in need of help will result in empathic concern, an important instigator for helping behavior.

An fMRI study of caring vs self-focus during induced compassion and pride.
doi: 10.1093/scan/nsr045
By Simon-Thomas, Emiliana R.; Godzik, Jakub; Castle, Elizabeth; Antonenko, Olga; Ponz, Aurelie; Kogan, Aleksander; Keltner, Dacher J.
Social Cognitive and Affective Neuroscience, Vol 7(6), Aug 2012, 635-648.
This study examined neural activation during the experience of compassion, an emotion that orients people toward vulnerable others and prompts caregiving, and pride, a self-focused emotion that signals individual strength and heightened status. Functional magnetic resonance images (fMRI) were acquired as participants viewed 55 s continuous sequences of slides to induce either compassion or pride, presented in alternation with sequences of neutral slides. Emotion self-report data were collected after each slide condition within the fMRI scanner. Compassion induction was associated with activation in the midbrain periaqueductal gray (PAG), a region that is activated during pain and the perception of others pain, and that has been implicated in parental nurturance behaviors. Pride induction engaged the posterior medial cortex, a region that has been associated with self-referent processing. Self-reports of compassion experience were correlated with increased activation in a region near the PAG, and in the right inferior frontal gyrus (IFG). Self-reports of pride experience, in contrast, were correlated with reduced activation in the IFG and the anterior insula. These results provide preliminary evidence towards understanding the neural correlates of important interpersonal dimensions of compassion and pride. Caring (compassion) and self-focus (pride) may represent core appraisals that differentiate the response profiles of many emotions.

Chapter 6:

Visiting women in prison: Who visits and who cares.
doi: 10.1300/J076v34n03_05
By Casey-Acevedo, Karen; Bakken, Tim
Journal of Offender Rehabilitation, Vol 34(3), 2002, 67-83.
Provides a descriptive analysis of visitation at a maximum security prison for women. Women inmates, including those in this study, are

young, single, unemployed, and undereducated. This study collected and examined visitation data on 222 women who averaged 22 mo of incarceration. During their incarceration, 79% of the women received at least one visit from a friend or family member. Of the women who received visits, the most frequent visitors were friends (evenly divided among males and females), not family members. For all visitors, the major impediment to visitation was the distance that they, especially children, had to travel to reach the prison. Perhaps as a result, 61% of the women who were mothers did not receive any visits from their children. The study concluded that visitation and the separation that ensues when visits are terminated can be a harrowing experience for women inmates, especially those who are separated from their children. Nonetheless, visitation can help foster prison adjustment and lead to better societal adjustment after prison.

Investigating the functional anatomy of empathy and forgiveness.
doi: 10.1097/00001756-200108080-00029
By Farrow, Tom F. D.; Zheng, Ying; Wilkinson, Iain D.; Spence, Sean A.; Deakin, J. F. William; Tarrier, Nick; Griffiths, Paul D.; Woodruff, Peter W. R.
NeuroReport: For Rapid Communication of Neuroscience Research, Vol 12(11), Aug 2001, 2433-2438.
Examined the neural correlates of making empathic and forgivability judgments. Functional magnetic resonance imaging (MRI) was used to detect brain regions engaged by judging others' emotional states and the forgivability of their crimes. 10 21–51 yr olds read and made judgements based on social scenarios and a high level baseline task (social reasoning). Results show that both empathic and forgivability judgements activated the left superior frontal gyrus, orbitofrontal gyrus and precuneus. Empathic judgements also activated the left anterior middle temporal and left inferior frontal gyri, while forgivability judgements activated the posterior cingulate gyrus. It is concluded that empathic and forgivability judgements activate specific regions of the human brain, which the authors propose contribute to social cohesion.

Exposure to violence reduces empathetic responses to other's pain.
doi: 10.1016/j.bandc.2013.04.005
By Guo, Xiuyan; Zheng, Li; Wang, Hongyi; Zhu, Lei; Li, Jianqi; Wang, Qianfeng; Dienes, Zoltan; Yang, Zhiliang
Brain and Cognition, Vol 82(2), Jul 2013, 187-191.
Past researches showed that empathy for pain not only triggers a resonance mechanism between other and self, but also is modulated by contextual factors. Using functional magnetic resonance imaging, the present study demonstrated that short-term media violence exposure

reduced both pain ratings and also the activation of anterior insula and anterior mid-cingulate cortex to other's pain. Thus, violence exposure modulated empathic responses to other's pain based on a physiological desensitization.

Differential prefrontal gray matter correlates of treatment response to fluoxetine or cognitive-behavioral therapy in obsessive–compulsive disorder.
doi: 10.1016/j.euroneuro.2012.06.014
By Hoexter, Marcelo Q.; Dougherty, Darin D.; Shavitt, Roseli G.; D'Alcante, Carina C.; Duran, Fabio L. S.; Lopes, Antonio C.; Diniz, Juliana B.; Batistuzzo, Marcelo C.; Evans, Karleyton C.; Bressan, Rodrigo A.; Busatto, Geraldo F.; Miguel, Euripedes C.
European Neuropsychopharmacology, Vol 23(7), Jul 2013, 569-580.
Nearly one-third of patients with obsessive–compulsive disorder (OCD) fail to respond to adequate therapeutic approaches such as serotonin reuptake inhibitors and/or cognitive-behavioral therapy (CBT). This study investigated structural magnetic resonance imaging (MRI) correlates as potential pre-treatment brain markers to predict treatment response in treatment-naïve OCD patients randomized between trials of fluoxetine or CBT. Treatment-naïve OCD patients underwent structural MRI scans before randomization to a 12-week clinical trial of either fluoxetine or group-based CBT. Voxel-based morphometry was used to identify correlations between pretreatment regional gray matter volume and changes in symptom severity on the Yale–Brown Obsessive–Compulsive Scale (Y–BOCS). Brain regional correlations of treatment response differed between treatment groups. Notably, symptom improvement in the fluoxetine treatment group (n = 14) was significantly correlated with smaller pretreatment gray matter volume within the right middle lateral orbitofrontal cortex (OFC), whereas symptom improvement in the CBT treatment group (n = 15) was significantly correlated with larger pretreatment gray matter volume within the right medial prefrontal cortex (mPFC). No significant a priori regional correlations of treatment response were identified as common between the two treatment groups when considering the entire sample (n = 29). These findings suggest that pretreatment gray matter volumes of distinct brain regions within the lateral OFC and mPFC were differentially correlated to treatment response to fluoxetine versus CBT in OCD patients. This study further implicates the mPFC in the fear/anxiety extinction process and stresses the importance of lateral portions of the OFC in mediating fluoxetine's effectiveness in OCD.

Increased orbital frontal gray matter volume after cognitive behavioural therapy in paediatric obsessive compulsive disorder.
doi: 10.3109/15622975.2012.674215
By Huyser, Chaim; van den Heuvel, Odile A.; Wolters, Lidewij H.; de Haan, Else; Boer, Frits; Veltman, Dick J.
The World Journal of Biological Psychiatry, Vol 14(4), May 2013, 319-331.

Objectives: Identify differences in regional brain volume between medication-free pediatric OCD patients and controls and examine changes after cognitive behavioural therapy. Methods: We assessed 29 medication-free paediatric OCD patients (Age: M = 13.78 years; SD = 2.58; range 8.2–19.0) and 29 controls, matched on age and gender, with T1-weighted MR scans in a repeated measures, pre-post treatment design. Voxel based morphometry (VBM) following diffeomorphic anatomical registration through exponential lie algebra (DARTEL) was used to test voxel-wise for the effects of diagnosis and treatment on regional gray matter (GM) and white matter (WM) volumes. Results: After cognitive behavioural therapy, orbitofrontal GM and capsula externa WM increased in paediatric OCD relative to controls. In patients, changes in symptom severity (delta CY-BOCS) correlated positively with GM volume in the orbitofrontal cortex after treatment. Furthermore, before treatment, paediatric OCD patients, compared to the controls, showed larger GM volume in left frontal pole and left parietal cortex and larger WM volume in cingulum and corpus callosum. Conclusions: Our findings underscore the involvement of the ventral frontal-striatal circuit in paediatric OCD and the plasticity of this circuit in response to the modulatory effects of CBT. The possible relation to brain development is discussed.

Oxytocin selectively increases perceptions of harm for victims but not the desire to punish offenders of criminal offenses.
doi: 10.1093/scan/nss026
By Krueger, Frank; Parasuraman, Raja; Moody, Lara; Twieg, Peter; de Visser, Ewart; McCabe, Kevin; O'Hara, Martin; Lee, Mary R.
Social Cognitive and Affective Neuroscience, Vol 8(5), Jun 2013, 494-498.

The neuropeptide oxytocin functions as a hormone and neurotransmitter and facilitates complex social cognition and approach behavior. Given that empathy is an essential ingredient for third-party decision-making in institutions of justice, we investigated whether exogenous oxytocin modulates empathy of an unaffected third-party toward offenders and victims of criminal offenses. Healthy male participants received intranasal oxytocin or placebo in a randomized, double-blind, placebo-controlled, between-subjects design. Participants were given a set of legal vignettes that described an event during which an offender engaged in criminal offenses against victims. As an unaffected third-party, participants were asked to rate those criminal offenses on the degree to which the offender deserved punishment and how much harm was inflicted on the victim. Exogenous oxytocin selectively increased third-party decision-makers' perceptions of harm for victims but not the desire to punish offenders of criminal offenses. We argue that oxytocin promoted empathic concern for the victim, which in turn increased the tendency for prosocial approach behavior regarding the interpersonal relationship between an unaffected third-party and a fictional victim in the criminal scenarios. Future research should explore the context- and person-dependent nature of exogenous oxytocin in individuals with antisocial personality disorder and psychopathy, in whom deficits in empathy feature prominently.

To Forgive or Not to Forgive: Emotional Costs and Benefits
doi: 10.1037/e413792005-835
By Vanderlaan, Kelly L.; Bauer, David J.; vanOyen Witvliet, Charlotte
Program of the Seventy-Second Annual Meeting; May 4-6, 2000; 204 [Midwestern Psychological Association (MPA)].
We examined the emotional effects of imagining two unforgiving (hurt, grudge) and two forgiving (empathy, forgiveness) responses to real-life offenders. Seventy-one participants completed 8 counterbalanced imagery trials of each condition in this within-subjects design. Participants rated feeling more aroused, more negative, less positive, and less in control during unforgiving imagery.

Appendix B
Information on some international organizations:

Feeding the hungry:
"101 Organizations to watch in 2014"that are trying to end world hunger (retrieved from http://foodtank.org/news/2014/01/one-hundred-one-organizations-to-watch-in-2014)

ACTION AGAINST HUNGER|ACF INTERNATIONAL— Recognized as a leader in the fight against malnutrition, ACF International runs programs in over 40 countries.

AFRICAN BIODIVERSITY NETWORK—This regional network was established in 1996 to preserve Africa's biodiversity. African Biodiversity Network educates and engages citizens in developing healthy communities based on biological, cultural, and spiritual diversity.

AFRICAN WOMEN IN AGRICULTURAL RESEARCH AND DEVELOPMENT (AWARD)—Launched in 2008, AWARD is a mentorship program in which top female agricultural scientists team up with smallholder female farmers in sub-Saharan Africa.

AFRICA RICE CENTER—Africa Rice Center aims to contribute to poverty alleviation and food security in Africa through research and development. One of the major tasks of the Africa Rice Center is the advancement and introduction of rice varieties that create resilience in agriculture.

AG INNOVATIONS NETWORK—Part of Ag Innovations Network's mission is to bring people together to create a better food system. With a deep interest in sustainable agriculture, Ag Innovations Network creates opportunities for individuals and communities to understand what needs to change to create a better future for food and farming.

AGRICULTURAL RESEARCH FOR DEVELOPMENT IN AFRICA (IITA)—IITA seeks to increase agricultural production in a sustainable way to help improve the nutritional status and well-being of people in sub-Saharan Africa.

ARCADIA CENTER FOR SUSTAINABLE FOOD AND AGRICULTURE—Arcadia is dedicated to creating a more equitable and sustainable local food system in the Washington, D.C. metropolitan area. In addition to a farm on the historic grounds of Woodlawn

Estate in Alexandria, Virginia, the Center has a Mobile Market, a 28-foot rolling farm stand that serves nine neighborhoods in D.C., Maryland, and Virginia.

ASHOKA — Ashoka operates worldwide (3,000 Ashoka Fellows in 70 countries) with private, philanthropic and citizen sector players to provide start-up financing, professional support services, and connections to a global network across the business and social sectors in the interest of social entrepreneurship. Their Nutrients for All program emphasizes the importance of improving nutrient density in food and agriculture.

AVRDC-THE WORLD VEGETABLE CENTER — This 41 year old organization is at the forefront of highlighting why everyone should eat their vegetables. With regional centers in Taiwan, Tanzania, Thailand, India, Uzbekistan, and Fiji, The World Vegetable Center works to improve not only nutrition, but incomes for small-scale farmers.

AUSTRALIAN CENTER FOR INTERNATIONAL AGRICULTURE RESEARCH (ACIAR) — ACIAR is part of the Australian Aid Program, the Center encourages Australia's agricultural scientists to use their skills for the benefit of developing countries as well as Australia.

AUSTRALIAN FOOD SOVEREIGNTY ALLIANCE — When Australia's Labor Party committed itself to creating a National Food Policy, the citizens responded with this alliance. The alliance was incorporated in 2012 with a nine-member managing committee. Today, the AFSA works with policy-makers to ensure fair balance and true representations of citizens' food interests.

BIOVERSITY INTERNATIONAL — Bioversity International provides scientific evidence of the important role of on-farm and wild agricultural and forest biodiversity in building a more nutritious, resilient, productive, and adaptable food and agricultural system.

BREAD FOR THE WORLD INSTITUTE — Bread for the World is an organization dedicated to ending hunger in the U.S. and around the world. Bread for the World uses their voice to change policies, programs, and conditions of hunger.

CENTER FOR FOOD SAFETY (CFS) — CFS, a national non-profit and advocacy organization, seeks to curb the use of harmful chemicals and practices in agriculture.

CENTER FOR HEALTH AND THE GLOBAL ENVIRONMENT HARVARD UNIVERSITY — The Health and Sustainable Food Program at the Center is working to inform eaters and institutions about the impact of their diets. Led by chef and National Geographic Society Explorer, Barton Seaver, the Center is working to "promote healthier people, more secure food supplies, and thriving communities."

CHANGE FOOD — Change Food's vision is to help shift the U.S. food supply to a regional, sustainable food system where healthy, nutritious food is accessible to all.

THE CHRISTENSEN FUND — Founded in 1957, The Christensen Fund is a cultural ally for indigenous groups around the world. The Fund seeks to establish partnerships and implement the United Nations Declaration of the Rights of Indigenous Peoples, as well as highlight the importance of indigenous and traditional crops.

CHICAGO COUNCIL ON GLOBAL AFFAIRS GLOBAL AGRICULTURE & FOOD PROGRAM — The program promotes discourse on global agriculture issues and produces the Global Food for Thought news brief to provide updated information, commentary, and analysis on global agricultural development and related issues.

CITY HARVEST — City Harvest collects excess food from all segments of the food industry and delivers it to 500 community food programs throughout New York City. The organization also serves to educate the public on food issues ranging from sustainable agriculture to diet-based disease prevention.

COALITION OF IMMOKALEE WORKERS (CIW) — CIW is a human rights organization addressing the issues of farm labor abuse, and improving farm worker conditions and wages.

COMMUNITY FOR ZERO HUNGER — Sustainable food sources require community action. The Community for Zero Hunger is designed to be the community-based arm of the United Nations Zero Hunger Challenge. The Community is a central repository of international agencies, government and institutional academic research — all geared toward meeting the Zero Hunger Challenge.

ECOAGRICULTURE PARTNERS — Built to support rural livelihoods, conserve biodiversity, and create sustainable solutions, EcoAgriculture has both a conservation and development strategy. The Landscapes for People, Food, and Nature Initiative provides research in 13 landscape sites around the world.

EDIBLE COMMUNITIES — Edible Communities is a publishing and information services company that creates editorially rich, community-based, local-foods publications in distinct culinary regions throughout the U.S. and Canada.

EDIBLE SCHOOLYARD — Edible Schoolyard evolved from the Chez Panisse Foundation, and the project serves as a model for the integration of gardening, cooking, and preparing sustainable food into core academic curriculum for public schools.

ENVIRONMENTAL WORKING GROUP (EWG) — A health and advocacy organization, the EWG works to produce the insight, through research, that spurs partnering organizations to create a healthier and cleaner environment and a more sustainable food system.

FAIR FOOD NETWORK (FFN) — FFN is based off the belief that everyone has the fundamental right to healthy, fresh, and sustainably grown food. FFN works to provide access to food, especially in underserved communities by implementing model programs and bringing people together.

FARM LABOR ORGANIZING COMMITTEE (FLOC) — Brokered in the mid 1960s to cooperate for common gain, the FLOC operates on two key principles: farmworkers need a unionized voice and all parties need to be part of the conversation. FLOC works to improve labor and housing conditions and to increase wages through collective bargaining agreements.

FEEDING THE 5000 — A global campaign designed to inspire communities to consider the costs of wasted food, Feeding the 5K works at the international level to create solutions in the area of food waste. Feeding the 5K is also leading the cause behind The Gleaning Network — an initiative to save wasted English fruits and veggies.

FOOD+TECH CONNECT — Food + Tech Connect, brings together the leading thinkers and do-ers in the food, agriculture, health, and technology industries to build a network of innovators to transform the business of food.

FOOD, AGRICULTURE, AND NATURAL RESOURCES POLICY ANALYSIS NETWORK (FANRPAN) — FANRPAN 's goal is to free Africa of hunger and poverty. FANRPAN objectives are to promote the development of appropriate agricultural policies in order to reduce poverty, enhance food security in Africa, and promote sustainable agricultural development in Africa.

FOOD AND WATER WATCH (FWW)—FWW works to ensure the food, water, and fish consumers eat is safe, accessible, and sustainable. Their website provides information to eaters, advocates, and activists to make change in the food system.

FOODCORPS—FoodCorps is a public private partnership that places emerging leaders in limited-resource communities to teach kids about what healthy food is and where it comes from.

FOOD DEMOCRACY NOW (FDN)—FDN is a grassroots movement of 650,000 farmers and citizens across the United States advocating for locally produced food and equal access to quality food. FDN aims to recreate regional food systems, supporting the growth of humane, natural and organic farms, and protecting the environment.

FOOD FOR LIFE—This project is active in over 60 countries worldwide. Food for Life volunteers serve more than three million, free, plant-based meals every day.

FOOD FOR THE HUNGRY (FH)—FH is a Christian organization dedicated to serving the poor for over 40 years. FH addresses hunger through short-term emergency relief as well as long term programs in more than 20 countries.

FOOD RECOVERY NETWORK—A few years ago, a group of enterprising University of Maryland students decided to take action and launched this initiative with the goal of delivering cafeteria leftovers to local food shelters. It has since expanded to 11 chapters on campuses across the U.S. Students involved in the Food Recovery Network visit their campus dining halls nightly to rescue leftover food and deliver it to local shelters and food pantries.

FOOD & ENVIRONMENT REPORTING NETWORK (FERN)—The Food & Environment Reporting Network is a non-profit news organization producing investigative reporting on food, agriculture, and environmental health.

FOOD FIRST/INSTITUTE FOR FOOD & DEVELOPMENT POLICY—Food First, a food system think tank, works to augment social movements in the fight for food security. Food First was founded in 1975 and works to inform eaters, farmers, and policymakers about local solutions to global food issues.

FOOD MYTHBUSTERS—Food MythBusters is working to tell the real story of how food is produced through short films. Through collaborations with different individuals and organizations, Food Mythbusters is proving that we can have a food system that is truly affordable, delicious, fair, and good for the planet.

FOOD USE FOR SOCIAL INNOVATION BY OPTIMISING WASTE PREVENTION STRATEGIES (FUSIONS)—FUSIONS hopes to tackle the issue of food waste throughout the supply chain, working with farmers and retailers to make sure less-than-perfect-looking produce isn't wasted. And they work with grocery stores to offer discounts to consumers on products that are nearing their expiration dates.

GLOBAL ALLIANCE FOR IMPROVED NUTRITION (GAIN)—GAIN is an alliance driven to end malnutrition created in 2002 at a U.N. Special Session of the UN General Assembly on Children. GAIN promotes public-private partnerships and has worked with 600 companies and civil society organisations in more than 30 countries, reaching an estimated 667 million people with nutritionally enhanced food products.

GLOBAL CROP DIVERSITY TRUST—Global Crop Diversity Trust is an independent international organization working to guarantee the conservation of crop diversity around the world.

GLOBAL FOODBANKING NETWORK—The Global FoodBanking Network works to support and enhance existing food banks and create new food bank systems around the world.

GLOBAL FORUM ON AGRICULTURAL RESEARCH (GFAR)—GFAR seeks to be the nexus of discussion concerning the future of agriculture. Focusing on global advocacy, institutions for the future, partnerships, and the spread of knowledge, GFAR provides a connection between scientific research and farming methods.

GROW BIOINTENSIVE/ECOLOGY ACTION—The organization educates and trains farmers around the world to establish high-yielding, sustainable agriculture systems that emphasize local food production and culturally appropriate techniques. Grow Biointensive farming techniques have been adopted in Mexico, Kenya, Argentina, Ecuador, Russia, Uzbekistan, the U.S., and other parts of the world. The organization also provides workshops and research publications.

GROWING POWER—Growing Power was founded by former pro-basketball player Will Allen and engages youth and people from diverse backgrounds by helping to provide equal access to healthy, high-quality, safe, and affordable food.

HANDS FOR HUNGER—Hands for Hunger is committed to eliminating unnecessary hunger and reducing food waste through creating partnerships within Bahamian communities, and developing food recovery and education projects.

HEIFER INTERNATIONAL—Heifer International has been working for more than 70 years in communities around the world, helping farmers practice better animal husbandry and develop more environmentally sustainable sources of food production.

INTERNATIONAL FOOD POLICY RESEARCH INSTITUTE (IFPRI)—Since the early 1970s, IFPRI has sought to improve the understanding of national agricultural and food policies to promote adoption of innovations in agricultural technology. In May, they'll be bringing together advocates, researchers, scientists, and policy makers from all over the world at their Building Resilience for Food and Nutrition Security conference in Ethiopia.

INSTITUTE FOR AGRICULTURE AND TRADE POLICY (IATP)—The Institute works to counter globalization, builds innovative economic models, and monitors overuse of agricultural antibiotics. They are also encouraging eaters, farmers, and policy-makers to think beyond the next Farm Bill and focus on better food policies.

INTERNATIONAL FUND FOR AGRICULTURAL DEVELOPMENT (IFAD)—A specialized agency of the United Nations, IFAD was established in 1977. The fund was designed to finance development projects for food production in developing countries. IFAD works directly with rural poverty groups to raise income levels and to eliminate hunger and malnutrition.

INTERNATIONAL LAND COALITION (ILC)—ILC is an alliance of civil society and intergovernmental organizations promoting equal access to land for women and men around the world by creating awareness and education.

INTERNATIONAL WATER MANAGEMENT INSTITUTE (IWMI)—IWMI is a non-profit organization that focuses their research on improving how water and land resources are managed with the aim of improving food security and reducing poverty while safeguarding water supplies.

JAMES BEARD FOUNDATION — Renowned author and teacher, James Beard was an avid culinary educator. The James Beard Foundation continues in his honor. By looking at food issues from a breadth of perspectives: economic, political, entertainment, and culture, the Foundation works to prove that food's meaning extends far beyond the plate.

JAMIE OLIVER'S FOOD REVOLUTION — With a central goal of fighting obesity, Food Revolution is urging Americans — and especially schools — to rethink the American diet. Oliver suggests teaching kids how to cook and urges parents to find out what their kids are eating at school.

LAST MINUTE MARKET (LMM) — LMM works with farmers, processing centers, grocery stores, and other food sellers to reclaim food that would have otherwise been wasted. Founded by Andrea Segrè, LMM now runs food donation programs in more than 40 Italian communities.

LA VIA CAMPESINA — La Via Campesina ("The International peasant's voice"), was established in 1993 as a network of small-scale agriculturalists. Comprised of 150 local groups from 70 countries, LVC represents close to 200 million farmers. LVC works to encourage small farmers to pursue local solutions to their regional food sustainability issues.

LANDESA RURAL DEVELOPMENT INSTITUTE — Landesa was created for the more than two billion people who live on less that US$2.00 a day. The organization works with governments in developing countries to implement policies and programs that ensure better land rights.

LEOPOLD CENTER FOR SUSTAINABLE AGRICULTURE — The Leopold Center is a research and education center at Iowa State University. The Center works to identify and reduce the negative environmental and social impacts of agriculture, while developing more sustainable ways to farm and protect the environment.

LOVE FOOD HATE WASTE (LFHW) — LFHW works to educate the public on how to reduce food waste in day-to-day activities. The program is funded under the Waste and Resources Action Programme (WRAP) in England, Northern Ireland, Scotland, and Wales, and provides cooking strategies and recipes aimed at minimizing food waste.

MORE AND BETTER — Established in 2003, More and Better is a complementary network built to support social movements, civil society and a core group of national unified campaigns resolved to fight against poverty and hunger. More and Better members define the level of support needed, lobby decision makers, and facilitate international practice exchange.

NATIONAL FAMILY FARM COALITION (NFFC) — NFFC is a North American organization which represents family farms and rural groups who face economic challenges of rural communities. NFFC collaborates with international and domestic organizations who share their goal — to promote a secure, economically stable, healthy, and safe food system.

NATIVE SEEDS/SEARCH — This organization conserves, distributes, and documents seed diversity as well as the role these seeds play in cultures of the American Southwest and northwest Mexico.

NATURAL RESOURCES DEFENSE COUNCIL (NRDC) — With more than 1.4 million members, NRDC is a staunch defender of Earth's resources. Their ground-breaking work on food waste in the U.S. is helping consumers and retailers save money and protect the environment.

OAKLAND INSTITUTE — An independent policy think tank, Oakland Institute works to create research in eight key areas: land rights, high food prices, sustainable food systems, foreign investments, international aid, trade agreements, climate change and poverty. It is Oakland Institute's key mission to increase public participation and encourage fair debate in each area.

OLDWAYS — Oldways is an advocate for healthier eating by educating the public about the benefits of traditional cooking embracing culture and heritage.

ONE ACRE FUND — One Acre Fund has developed an innovative model to help farmers improve yields by providing them credit for farm inputs, providing those inputs within walking distance of their farms, and making sure that farmers are able to sell their harvest at a profit. By 2020, the organization will serve 1.4 million farm families.

OXFAM — Oxfam is a confederation of 17 organizations working together to find lasting solutions to poverty and injustice. Oxfam works to find practical, innovative ways for people to lift themselves out of poverty and thrive. Oxfam America's recent Behind the Brands campaign is highlighting how some of consumers favorite brands have hidden costs — to farmers, food security, and the environment.

PARTNERS IN HEALTH (PIH) — PIH's mission is to provide a preferential option for the poor in health care. With offices in more than ten countries, PIH provides medical treatment and food supplements to malnourished children.

POSTHARVEST EDUCATION FOUNDATION — Postharvest offers training materials, e-learning programs, and mentoring opportunities that help farmers around the world prevent food loss. Their postharvest management guide is available in ten languages, featuring topics such as how to choose the best time for harvest and the advantages of different transportation methods.

PROLINNOVA — Prolinnova is an NGO-initiated multistakeholder program working to promote local innovation in sustainable agriculture. They focus on indigenous and traditional knowledge work to promote resilience among farmers, pastoralists, and fisherfolk. Among its many goals, the organization is working to highlight the importance of participatory research and build stronger farmer-extension-researcher partnerships.

RAINFOREST ALLIANCE — The Alliance works to protect biodiversity and ensure sustainable livelihoods by transforming land-use and farming techniques, business practices, and consumer behavior. Their vision is "a world where people and the environment prosper."

REAL FOOD CHALLENGE (RFC) — Started in 2008, RFC is a mobilization of mainly students advocating for the shift of US$1 billion of existing university food budgets away from industrial farms and junk food and, instead, toward local and community-based, fair, ecologically sound, and humane food sources by 2020.

RE:CHAR — Re:char uses innovative technology to help farmers grow more food. They develop and deploy small biochar production system in the developing world to increase farmers' yields.

RESTAURANT OPPORTUNITY CENTERS (ROC) — ROC's mission is to improve the wages and working conditions for the U.S. restaurant workforce. Since it's founding, ROC has successfully conducted restaurant justice campaigns, provided job training and placement, opened its own cooperative restaurant, and conducted research and policy work.

RODALE INSTITUTE — The Rodale Institute is a non-profit dedicated to pioneering organic farming through research and outreach. For more than 60 years, Rodale Institute has been researching the best practices of organic agriculture and sharing their findings with farmers and scientists throughout the world. They advocate for policies that support farmers, and teach consumers organic agriculture is good for both people and the planet.

RURAL WOMEN MAKING CHANGE (RWMC) — RWMC is a Community University Research Alliance (CURA) in Canada that supports rural women's projects for change in three areas — women's organizations' day to day work; women's and girl's everyday experience; and gender and rural policy in trans-local arenas.

SAVE FOOD FROM THE FRIDGE — Jihyun Ryou, Korean designer and expert on food preservation, launched this project that attempts to prevent waste in homes. She outlines several ideas for keeping foods fresher longer without the use of modern kitchen technologies. In addition, she has also created a collaborative blog where anyone can submit their own innovative food storage ideas.

SAVORY INSTITUTE — The Savory Institute was founded in 2009, to combat climate change and environmental degradaton by teaching sustainable, holistic grazing practices to farmers and ranchers worldwide.

SCALING UP NUTRITION — Scaling Up Nutrition is a worldwide organization that works with national leaders to incorporate nutrition into all development decisions with a core focus on empowering women.

SEED SAVERS EXCHANGE — Seed Savers Exchange is dedicated to the saving and sharing of organic, heirloom, and non-GMO seeds.

SOIL ASSOCIATION — Founded in 1946, the Soil Association works to ensure that organic systems are being used whenever possible. The Association encourages new solutions to climate change, improvements to animal welfare and greater biodiversity support. The Food for Life Partnership teams up with local schools to transform dietary choices of thousands of young students.

SLOW FOOD INTERNATIONAL — Designed to counter fast food and fast life, this 100,000 member-supported association takes on biodiversity projects, food education and connects young people through the Slow Food Youth Network. Slow Food works on three interconnected principles: good diet that is part of local culture; clean food production; and fair consumer prices.

SUSTAINABLE FOOD TRUST—With the belief that everyone is in a position to influence a change, Sustainable Food Trust works to enhance production of quality foods. Through research and by examining the close relationship between farmers, consumers, industry-leaders and policy-makers, the Trust takes a closer look at what needs to be done to improve the food system.

STONE BARNES CENTER FOR FOOD AND AGRICULTURE—Located just 25 miles from Manhattan, New York, Stone Barnes Center is a non-profit farm institution. With goals of creating healthy and sustainable food systems, Stone Barnes Center works to increase public awareness of sustainable choices, train farmers environmentally techniques, and educate youth of farming choices.

TEDX MANHATTAN—TEDx is a program of local, self-organized events that bring people together to share deep discussion. TEDxManhattan is organizing "Changing the Way We Eat," led by Diane Hatz, founder and executive director of Change Food, to help bolster and create news ideas in the sustainable food movement.

THE COOKBOOK PROJECT—The CookBook Project trains local leaders worldwide to use food culture and cooking program curriculum in their own communities. The goal is "to empower youth worldwide to cook REAL food with family and friends to reverse the global obesity and chronic disease epidemic."

THE HUNGER PROJECT—The Hunger Project works in partnership with grassroots organizations in Africa, Asia and Latin America to develop effective bottom-up strategies empowering people to overcome hunger and poverty. Programs teach self-reliance and foster partnerships with the local government.

THINK.EAT.SAVE.—A campaign of the Save Food Initiative, this partnership supports the United Nations Zero Hunger Challenge. Think.Eat.Save takes a closer look at food production and how much is lost and wasted at each step of the production process.

THOUSAND GARDENS—Thousand Gardens in Africa is a project under the Slow Food Foundation for Biodiversity that is working to cultivate more than 1,000 food gardens in schools, villages and on the outskirts of cities in 25 African countries.

TRANSFORM NUTRITION—A consortium of six organizations, Transform Nutrition pushes nutrition up higher on the political agenda and works to create more effective action to improve nutrition.

UNION OF CONCERNED SCIENTISTS — The Union of Concerned Scientists works to ensure that all people have clean air and energy, as well as safe and sufficient food. UCS combines technical analysis and effective advocacy to create innovative, practical solutions for a healthy, safe, and sustainable future.

WALLACE CENTER AT WINROCK INTERNATIONAL — The Center serves the growing community of civic, business, and philanthropic organizations involved in building a good food system in the United States. The organization is working to advance regional efforts for a healthy, green, fair, affordable food system into larger scale markets to benefit more producers, consumers, and businesses.

WHYHUNGER — WhyHunger is a leader in building the movement to end hunger and poverty by connecting people to nutritious, affordable food and by supporting grassroots solutions that inspire self-reliance and community empowerment.

WOMEN, FOOD AND AGRICULTURE NETWORK (WFAN) — WFAN is a community of women involved in sustainable agriculture, working primarily in the U.S. Midwest, and exists to give female farmers the opportunity to exchange information, support, and help each other in creating a sustainable food system.

WOMEN FOR WOMEN INTERNATIONAL — This organization works in eight conflict zone countries to provide women survivors of war tools and resources to become self sufficient. This includes; breadmaking, caring for livestock, and farming.

WORLD AGROFORESTRY CENTRE (ICRAF) — ICRAF is an international institute headquartered in Nairobi, Kenya that specializes in the sustainable management, protection, and regulation of tropical rainforest and natural forest reserves.

WORLD FARMER'S ORGANIZATION (WFO) — WFO is an international organization "of farmers for farmers," to bring together farmers with the goal of developing policies that favor farmers around the world, particularly smallholder farmers.

WORLD FOOD PROGRAMME (WFP) SCHOOL MEALS — WFP School Meal's vision is to reduce hunger among schoolchildren so that hunger is not an obstacle to their development. WFP provides meals to around 22 million children in 60 countries, often in the hardest-to-reach areas.

WORLD RESOURCES INSTITUTE—WRI is a global research organization working closely with leaders to turn big ideas. According to their research, the world will have to close a gap of nearly 70 percent between the amount of food available today and that will be required in 2050. WRI is researching ways to reduce agriculture's impact on climate, ecosystems, and water to secure a sustainable food future.

WORLD RURAL FORUM—A liaison between research centers and cause-driven associations, the WRF is a forum for issues of rural development. The organization defines itself as a network, covering five continents. It believes its duty is to facilitate fruitful interaction between different agents in rural environments.

*****

Giving water to the thirsty.
Organizations that are trying to end world water shortage:
"Here are over 80 organizations (community, academic, governmental, funding, and more) working on water and sanitation issues in multiple countries around the world. Organizations were chosen for this list if they work in two or more countries globally. (Retrieved from http://waterfortheages.org/international-water-organizations/)

AFRICAN MINISTERS' COUNCIL ON WATER—The African Ministers' Council on Water (AMCOW) was formed in 2002 in Abuja Nigeria, primarily to promote cooperation, security, social and economic development and poverty eradication among member states through the effective management of the continent's water resources and provision of water supply services.

ALTERNATIVE WORLD WATER FORUM—Over 150 organizations (trade unions, water-users', environmental, humanitarian and alter-mondialist associations, NGOs from thirty different countries and international networks), in addition to hundreds of people, have already signed the declaration of the participants issued at the conclusion of the Alternative World Water Forum. Please share its ideas, make the declaration widely known, sign it and get others to sign it, so that the current in favour of water as a commons can become overpoweringly strong!

AMMAN IMMAN—Amman Imman is dedicated to improving and saving lives among the poorest and most abandoned populations of the world, by supplying permanent sources of water in the Azawak of West Africa. "Water is Life." This could not be truer than in the Azawak of West Africa where half a million people have no water for ten months of the year. Only half of the children reach their fifth birthday, and many simply die of thirst. They are the human faces of climate change.

ANN CAMPANA JUDGE FOUNDATION — The Ann Campana Judge Foundation (hereinafter referred to as the ACJF) honors Ann Campana Judge, former Travel Department Head of The National Geographic Society, who was murdered by terrorists on September 11, 2001, just a few months short of her 50th birthday. She was aboard American Airlines Flight 77, which was crashed into the Pentagon. She was a world traveler, mainly to developing countries, and a great supporter of students and those less fortunate than herself. The ACJF will perpetuate her memory by promoting, undertaking, supporting and funding philanthropic projects in and relating to developing countries, especially those projects focused on water, health and sanitation, and featuring student involvement.

AUSAID — Hygiene promotion is one of the most effective health interventions but globally it has been under-resourced compared to funding for drinking water and sanitation. While many of Australia's water and sanitation programs include hygiene promotion, improved outcomes could be achieved by the increased use of methods that promote behaviour change within targeted communities.

BPD WATER AND SANITATION — BPD (Building Partnerships for Development in Water and Sanitation) is a non-profit charity that improves the provision of water and sanitation services in unserved and poorly served communities by ensuring that partnerships are effective and appropriately ambitious.

CARE — CARE helps communities build and maintain clean water systems and latrines. Both directly and through local organizations, CARE provides training and subsidizes construction, but communities make significant contributions in cash and labor, and pay the cost of operation and maintenance. The goal of these projects is to reduce the health risks of water-related diseases and to increase the earning potential of households by saving time otherwise spent gathering water. Projects also include educating people about good hygiene habits to reduce the risk of illnesses.

CAWST — CAWST, the Centre for Affordable Water and Sanitation Technology, is a non-profit organization that provides training and consulting to organizations that work directly with populations in developing countries who lack access to clean water and basic sanitation. CAWST "walks beside" hundreds of organizations — government agencies, community groups, and local and international NGOs of all sizes — in 63 countries as they develop their capacities to deliver water and sanitation programs locally.

CHARITY: WATER — Charity: Water is a non-profit organization bringing clean and safe drinking water to people in developing nations.

CIRCLE OF BLUE — Circle of Blue is an international network of journalists, scholars and citizens that connects humanity to the global freshwater crisis. A project of the non-profit Pacific Institute, America's premier water policy think tank, Circle of Blue pioneers communications and information technology with a new model for moving vital issues into the mainstream. It inspires and informs decision making with original reporting, dynamic data spaces and engaging social media.

CLEARWATER INITIATIVE — ClearWater Initiative is a non-governmental charitable organization that strives to provide clean, potable water solutions to populations in need. Within 5 years, ClearWater's vision is to provide access to potable water to 50,000 people. Within 10 years ClearWater will provide clean water to 250,000 people in need. We also hope to begin offering seed grants for simple, innovative projects in complex humanitarian emergencies shortly. The purpose of these small grants will be to provide seed funding for relief professionals looking to develop projects that will advance technical aspects of international disaster response, with an emphasis on provision of essential services for refugees and internally displaced populations. Grant applications will come on-line as soon as we have sufficient funds to support the program.

DFID UK — We will help to provide access to clean drinking water, improve access to effective sanitation and provide basic hygiene education (eg hand washing and the dangers of open defecation) for 60 million people by 2015. The majority will be people who live in rural areas as well as women and girls. One way we will do this is by building stand pipes and pumps in and around villages. We will also build toilets and sewage systems and inform people of the benefits of good hygiene practices, to stop them getting sick and dying from preventable diseases. We will help governments, citizens and the private sector in developing countries to manage water resources better. This will give more families, farmers and businesses access to the water they need, when they need it. We will research methods of improving water security and management of existing water resources, as well as exploring new approaches to improve access to water, sanitation and hygiene for people in developing countries.

DIGDEEP WATER — DIGDEEP field projects always establish local water councils: groups of 8-10 villagers who care for a new water source. Their input and decision-making ensure each project's long term sustainability. Here at home, our own Water Council has a similar function. The Water Council is an exclusive group of "venture philanthropists" — quarterly donors that believe so strongly in our life saving mission, that they're happy to cover our operational costs.

EUROPEAN WATER PARTNERSHIP — The European Water Partnership (EWP) is an independent value based non-profit organization structured as an open and inclusive member association. The EWP harnesses European capacity, helps to coordinate initiatives and activities in international water issues and undertakes worldwide promotion of European expertise related to water. The ultimate goal of the EWP is to elaborate strategies and implement concrete actions to achieve the objectives of the Water Vision for Europe.

EUROPEAN WATER INITIATIVE — In 2002, at the World Summit for Sustainable Development in Johannesburg, we launched the "European Union Water Initiative" EUWI-Water for Life. The goal? "To create the conditions for mobilising all available EU resources (human & financial), and to coordinate them to achieve the water-related Millennium Development Goals (MDGs) in partner countries."

FAO LAND AND WATER DEVELOPMENT DIVISION — The Land and Water Division aims at enhancing the agricultural productivity and advancing the sustainable use of land and water resources through their improved tenure, management, development and conservation. It addresses the challenges member countries face in ensuring productive and efficient use of land and water resources in order to meet present and future demands for agricultural products, while ensuring the long-term sustainability of the land and water quantity and quality. It promotes equitable access to these natural resources with a view to enhancing productivity, livelihoods and ecosystem services. It provides assistance to member nations in developing policies, programmes, best practices and tools in the fields of irrigation and drainage, soil conservation, drought mitigation, water rights, access to natural resources, and improvement of land markets.

FOOD AND WATER WATCH — Food and Water Watch works to ensure the food, water and fish we consume is safe, accessible and sustainably produced. So we can all enjoy and trust in what we eat and drink, we help people take charge of where their food comes from, keep clean, affordable, public tap water flowing freely to our homes, protect the environmental quality of oceans, force government to do its job protecting citizens, and educate about the importance of keeping shared resources under public control.

FRESH: FOCUSING RESOURCES ON EFFECTIVE SCHOOL HEALTH — "Education for All" means ensuring that all children have access to basic education of good quality. This implies creating an environment in schools and in basic education programmes in which children are both able and enabled to learn. Such an environment must be friendly and welcoming to children, healthy for children, effective with children, and protective of children. The development of such child-friendly learning environments is an essential part of the overall efforts by countries around the world to increase access to, and improve the quality, of their schools.

FRIENDS OF THE EARTH—MIDDLE EAST — Founded 1994. Formerly: Ecopeace. Promotes cooperative efforts to to protect the "shared environmental heritage" of the Middle East, focusing particularly on transboundary ecosystems such as the Dead Sea Basin, the Gulf of Aqaba, and the Eastern Mediterranean Sea. Members are groups in Egypt, Israel, Jordan, and Palestine. Affiliated with Friends of the Earth International.

GENDER AND WATER ALLIANCE — The mission of GWA is to promote women's and men's equitable access to and management of safe and adequate water, for domestic supply, sanitation, food security and environmental sustainability. GWA believes that equitable access to and control over water is a basic right for all, as well as a critical factor in promoting poverty eradication and sustainability.

GLOBAL HANDWASHING DAY — Global Handwashing Day 2010 will revolve around schools and children. On Global Handwashing Day, playgrounds, classrooms, community centers, and the public spaces of towns and cities will be awash with activity to drive handwashing behavior change on a scale never seen before, bringing the critical issue to center stage.

GLOBAL WATER — Global Water is an international, non-profit humanitarian organization focused on creating safe water supplies, sanitation facilities and related health programs for rural villagers in developing countries. We believe the lack of safe drinking and agricultural water and lack of access to sanitation facilities are the root causes of disease, hunger and poverty throughout the world today.

GLOBAL WATER CHALLENGE — A committed group of leading organizations has joined forces to catalyze transformational change in the water and sanitation sector through the Global Water Challenge (GWC). The GWC is an initiative to provide safe drinking water, sanitation and hygiene education to people who lack these basic services. Launched by a diverse coalition of corporations, foundations, and aid organizations, the GWC is a unique partnership to build healthy communities and provide sustainable solutions to ensure the availability of potable water for those in need. The goal of the GWC is to bring safe water and sanitation to millions by identifying and multiplying the solutions that work.

GLOBAL WATER PARTNERSHIP — GWP was founded in 1996 by the World Bank, the United Nations Development Programme (UNDP), and the Swedish International Development Cooperation Agency (SIDA) to foster integrated water resource management (IWRM).

GLOBAL GREEN USA — Global Green USA is a national environmental organization addressing three of the greatest challenges facing humanity. President Gorbachev founded the organization in order to create a new approach to solving the world's most pressing environmental challenges by reconnecting humanity to the environment.

H20 FOR LIFE — H20 for Life connects schools in the United States with schools in developing countries to complete WASH (WAter, Sanitation, and Hygiene) in Schools projects. A nonprofit, all-volunteer organization run by teachers, parents, and students, H20 for Life aims to help students build an allegiance to and an understanding of their partner school through curriculum and experiential learning while raising funds for WASH in Schools projects. 100 percent of contributions raised by schools goes directly to partner school projects. All overhead expenses are funded through in-kind donations and grants.

HEALING WATERS INTERNATIONAL — Healing Waters International is a nonprofit organization providing safe water solutions in communities where poverty is compounded by contaminated water.

INTERNATIONAL ASSOCIATION OF HYDRO-GEOLOGISTS — Founded 1956. Affiliated with the International Union of Geological

Sciences. Promotes international cooperation among groundwater scientists and engineers; encourages exchange of hydrogeological information to advance the science and study of groundwater and aquifers. Has commissions on Groundwater Protection and on Hydrogeology in Developing Nations. Members are individuals and institutions in some 135 countries.

INTERNATIONAL ASSOCIATION OF HYDROLOGICAL SCIENCES—Founded 1922. Affiliated with the International Union of Geodesy and Geophysics. "The oldest and foremost international non-governmental body dealing with hydrology and water resources." Promotes the study and discussion of scientific aspects of hydrology. Among IAHS's scientific units are the International Commission on Water Quality (ICWQ) and the International Commission on Water Resources Systems (ICWRS). Members of IAHS are national committees and individual hydrologists in many countries.

INTERNATIONAL COMMISSION ON LARGE DAMS—Founded 1928. Encourages improvements in the design, construction, maintenance, and operation of large dams through research and exchange of information. (Large dams are defined as dams over 15 meters high, of which there are over 36,000 in operation worldwide.) Main activity is a triennial congress. Members are national committees in 80 some countries.

INTERNATIONAL MEDICAL CORPS—International Medical Corps is a global, humanitarian, nonprofit organization dedicated to saving lives and relieving suffering through health care training and relief and development programs.

INTERNATIONAL OFFICE FOR WATER—Formed in 1991 by the merger of 3 groups. Promotes "capacity building for better water management." Develops exchanges and provides training and other services to European and developing countries in the areas of water resources, wastewater treatment, and prevention of water pollution. Provides the secretariat for the International Network of Basin Organizations, which includes over a hundred groups in some 40 countries. Members of IOWater are organizations in some 25 countries.

INTERNATIONAL RIVERS —International Rivers works to protect rivers and rights, and promote real solutions for meeting water, energy and flood management needs.

IRC INTERNATIONAL WATER AND SANITATION CENTRE — Formerly: International Reference Centre for Community Water Supply and Sanitation. Founded 1968. Provides information and documentation services, training, and research and development support to water supply and sanitation projects and programs in developing countries. Governing board includes representatives of UNICEF, UNDP, WHO, and the World Bank. Has partner organizations in Africa, Asia, and Latin America.

INTERNATIONAL WATER ASSOCIATION — Merger of the International Water Supply Association and the International Association on Water Quality. Promotes the "integrated management of water as the best strategy for securing safe water supplies and adequate sanitation for communities worldwide." Covers "all aspects of water supply and treatment; wastewater collection, treatment, and disposal; and overall management of water quality and quantity." Among its specialist groups on sources and effects of pollution are: Environmental Restoration; Eutrophication; Forest Industry; Groundwater; Hazard Assessment and Control of Environmental Contaminants; Landfill Management of Solid Wastes; and Surface Water. In addition, there are specialist groups on various treatment processes, management, and training. Members of IWA are individuals and organizations (agencies, firms, universities, and associations) in some 130 countries.

INTERNATIONAL OFFICE OF WATER — IOW has a network of partners, public and private organizations involved in the management and protection of water resources, in France, in Europe and in the World. The site mission of IOW is: Train, inform, manage and cooperate in the field of water.

INTERNATIONAL WATER RESOURCES ASSOCIATION — Founded 1972. "An interdisciplinary worldwide organization for water managers, scientists, planners, manufacturers, administrators, educators, lawyers, physicians, and others concerned with the future of our water resources." Members are individuals in over 100 countries.

JOINT MONITORING PROGRAM — The WHO/UNICEF Joint Monitoring Programme (JMP) for Water Supply and Sanitation is the official United Nations mechanism tasked with monitoring progress towards the Millennium Development Goal (MDG) relating to drinking-water and sanitation (MDG 7, Target 7c), which is to: "Halve, by 2015, the proportion of people without sustainable access to safe drinking-water and basic sanitation".

LIFEWATER — This is a christian, religious organization. Lifewater does not merely hire staff or consultants to drill wells, fix hand pumps, or transmit information to those in need. Rather, the goal is to train and equip nationals with the skills needed to access, use, and maintain safe water — and pass these skills along to others. Because our partners take ownership in the process, they are empowered to continue the work long after Lifewater volunteers have returned home.

LIVING WATER INTERNATIONAL — Living Water International exists to demonstrate the love of God by helping communities acquire desperately needed clean water, and to experience "living water" — the gospel of Jesus Christ — which alone satisfies the deepest thirst.

MERCY CORPS — Mercy Corps works amid disasters, conflicts, chronic poverty and instability to unleash the potential of people who can win against nearly impossible odds. Since 1979, Mercy Corps has provided $1.3 billion in assistance to people in 100 nations. Supported by headquarters offices in North America, Europe and Asia, the agency's unified global programs employ 3,400 staff worldwide and reach nearly 14.4 million people in more than 35 countries.

PACIFIC INSTITUTE — The Pacific Institute works to create a healthier planet and sustainable communities. They conduct interdisciplinary research and partner with stakeholders to produce solutions that advance environmental protection, economic development, and social equity — in California, nationally, and internationally.

PRACTICAL ACTION — Practical Action works alongside communities to find practical solutions to the poverty they face. We see technology as a vital contributor to people's livelihoods. Our definition of technology includes physical infrastructure, machinery and equipment, knowledge and skills and the capacity to organise and use all of these. We actively seek to work with communities and adopt a collaborative approach, sharing knowledge and experience. We increase our impact by scaling up success and pushing for policy change that directly benefits poor communities.

PURE WATER FOR THE WORLD — Pure Water, a non profit (501c3), helps the underserved in developing countries by providing safe drinking water, sanitation, and hygiene education. The goal of Pure Water for the World, Inc. is to prevent children from suffering from water borne diseases that cause pain and misery as a result of consuming contaminated water and improper hygiene habits. We do this by providing sustainable safe drinking water filtration systems, latrines and hygiene education to families and communities in developing countries.

RURAL WATER SUPPLY NETWORK—The Rural Water Supply Network (RWSN) is the global network of professionals and practitioners working to raise standards of knowledge and evidence, technical and professional competence, practice and policy in rural water supply and so fulfil the vision of sustainable rural water services for all. RWSN places a very strong emphasis on innovation, documentation, research and capacity building.

RYAN'S WELL FOUNDATION—The Ryan's Well Foundation grew from the commitment of one boy, Ryan Hreljac, who learned of the great need for clean and safe water in developing countries in his 1st grade class. With the support of friends, family and the community, Ryan raised enough money to build a well in Africa. In 1999, at age seven, Ryan's first well was built at Angolo Primary School in northern Uganda. To this day, the well continues to serve the community.

SANDEC—Sandec is the Department of Water and Sanitation in Developing Countries at the Swiss Federal Institute of Aquatic Science and Technology (Eawag). Our mandate is to develop concepts and technologies which are adapted to the various physical and socio-economic conditions prevailing in developing countries, sustainably insuring populations' access to improved water and sanitation.

SANITATION AND WATER FOR ALL—Sanitation and Water for All is a global partnership between developing countries, donors, multi-lateral agencies, civil society and other development partners working together to achieve universal and sustainable access to sanitation and drinking water, with an immediate focus on achieving the Millennium Development Goals in the most off-track countries. This transparent, accountable and results-oriented framework for action provides a common vision, values and principles that support a vision for everyone in the world to have sustainable access to sanitation and drinking water.

SUSTAINABLE SANITATION ALLIANCE—The Sustainable Sanitation Alliance (SuSanA) is an informal network of organisations who share a common vision on sustainable sanitation. SuSanA came into existence in early 2007 and works as a coordination platform, working platform, sounding board, contributor to the policy dialogue on sustainable sanitation and as a "catalyst". At the present time, the secretariat function is carried out by GIZ (German International Cooperation) and the current number of partners is displayed at the bottom of the website page.

SIWI—The Stockholm International Water Institute (SIWI) is a policy institute that seeks sustainable solutions to the world's escalating water crisis. SIWI manages projects, synthesises research and publishes findings and recommendations on current and future water, environment, governance and human development issues.

THE MILLENNIUM WATER ALLIANCE—These sobering facts inspire the Millennium Water Alliance (MWA), a consortium of leading nongovernmental organizations (NGOs), to strive toward our goal to help 500 million people obtain water and basic sanitation by 2015. Our vision mirrors our belief that no one should die or suffer chronic illness as the result of a water-related disease.

THE WATER TRUST—The Water Trust (TWT) is a 501(c)(3) non-profit working to improve water, sanitation and hygiene (WASH) in East Africa. Our mission is to combat disease and poverty in the developing world through sustainable investments in WASH. We have been working in Masindi District, Uganda since our formation in 2008. Note that we changed our name in 2012 from Busoga Trust America.

THE WORLD BANK-WATER—Meeting the increasing demands for water services, while managing water in a sustainable way can be a tremendous challenge for many countries. Water services (water supply and sanitation, irrigation and drainage, energy, environmental services) use water to promote growth and development, but water is finite and access to services is not guaranteed if they are not managed properly.

UNDP-MAINSTREAMING GENDER IN WATER MANAGE-MENT—The Guide is a reference document designed to facilitate access to available literature and resources regarding gender and IWRM; improve the sustainability and effectiveness of water-related activities through incorporation of gender equality and diversity; and improve understanding and awareness of gender concepts through an easy reference to existing materials, cases, and tools.

UNDP-WATER AND OCEAN GOVERNANCE—Through the earth's water cycle, the planet's fresh Water and Ocean are inextricably linked. Ninety-seven percent of the earth's water is in the ocean and the ocean supplies almost all the water that falls on land as rain and snow. Of the small portion that is freshwater, about a third is in groundwater and a mere 0.3% in accessible surface waters. Currently, just under 900 million people lack access to safe water and over 2.7 billion lack access to basic sanitation. The 2015 MDG for water is on target to be achieved globally, but with significant regional and national gaps, particularly in Sub-Saharan Africa. The impacts of low access to water and sanitation represent a substantial drag on socioeconomic development in many countries.

UNEP-GEMSTAT—The United Nations Global Environment Monitoring System (GEMS) Water Programme is dedicated to providing environmental water quality data and information of the highest integrity, accessibility and interoperability. These data are used in water assessments and capacity building initiatives around the world. GEMStat is designed to share surface and ground water quality data sets collected from the GEMS/Water Global Network, including more than 3,000 stations, close to four million records, and over 100 parameters.

UN-WATER—UN-Water strengthens coordination and coherence among UN entities dealing with issues related to all aspects of freshwater and sanitation. This includes surface and groundwater resources, the interface between freshwater and seawater and water-related disasters.

UNESCO-WORLD WATER ASSESSMENT PROGRAM—This UN-wide programme seeks to develop the tools and skills needed to achieve a better understanding of those basic processes, management practices and policies that will help improve the supply and quality of global freshwater resources.

UNESCO-IHE INSTITUTE FOR WATER EDUCATION—The UNESCO-IHE Institute for Water Education is established in 2003. It carries out research, education and capacity building activities in the fields of water, environment and infrastructure. UNESCO-IHE continues the work that began in 1957 when IHE first offered a postgraduate diploma course in hydraulic engineering to practising professionals from developing countries.

UNICEF-WASH—UNICEF works in more than 90 countries around the world to improve water supplies and sanitation facilities in schools and communities, and to promote safe hygiene practices. We sponsor a wide range of activities and work with many partners, including families, communities, governments and like-minded organizations. In emergencies we provide urgent relief to communities and nations threatened by disrupted water supplies and disease. All UNICEF WASH programmes are designed to contribute to the Millennium Development Goal for water and sanitation: to halve, by 2015, the proportion of people without sustainable access to safe water and basic sanitation.

USAID-ENVIRONMENTAL HEALTH—USAID's Environmental Health Team sponsors projects and provides financial support to selected governmental and international organizations to conduct programs and research on environmental health issues.

VOSS FOUNDATION—The Voss Foundation is a non-profit organization dedicated to providing access to clean water to communities in Sub-Saharan Africa and raising awareness of ongoing need in the region. The Voss Foundation aims to help fulfill communities' water requirements and then focus on the self-improvement of lives and communities once basic water needs are satisfied. We have a particular interest in assisting women and girls who, relieved of the burden of fetching water, have time to devote to education and enterprise.

WASH ADVOCATES—WASH Advocates is a nonprofit advocacy initiative in Washington DC entirely dedicated to helping solve the global safe drinking water, sanitation, and hygiene (WASH) challenge. Our mission is to increase awareness of the global WASH challenge and solutions, and to increase the amount and effectiveness of resources devoted to those solutions throughout the developing world.

WASH FUNDERS—With seed funding from the Conrad N. Hilton Foundation, and additional support from the Bill & Melinda Gates Foundation, the Rockefeller Foundation, and the Howard G. Buffett Foundation, the Foundation Center has developed WASHfunders.org as a "one stop shop" for funding and needs-related data and information for donors, policymakers, and other stakeholders interested in water, sanitation, and hygiene. With dynamically updated information, news, and knowledge relating to philanthropy and sustainable access to safe water, WASHfunders.org aims to facilitate better collaboration and more strategic decision-making among funders and seeks to raise awareness about water and the full WASH continuum among donors.

WATER AID—WaterAid and its partners use practical solutions to provide safe water, effective sanitation and hygiene education to the world's poorest people. We also seek to influence policy at national and international levels.

WATER AND SANITATION PROGRAM—The Water and Sanitation Program (WSP) is a multi-donor partnership administered by the

World Bank to support poor people in obtaining affordable, safe and sustainable access to water and sanitation services. We work directly with client governments at the local and national level in 25 countries through regional offices in Africa, East and South Asia, Latin America and the Caribbean, and in, Washington D.C.

WATER COLLECTIVE — Water Collective brings life lasting clean water to developing communities. Through robust solutions and economic empowerment, we keep clean water flowing for years to come.

WATER, ENGINEERING, AND DEVELOPMENT CENTER — WEDC is one of the world's leading education and research institutes for developing knowledge and capacity in water and sanitation for low- and middle-income countries. We are based in the School of Civil and Building Engineering at Loughborough University, one of the top award-winning Universities in the UK.

WATER FOR PEOPLE — Water For People helps people in developing countries improve their quality of life by supporting the development of locally sustainable drinking water resources, sanitation facilities and health and hygiene education programs.

WATER INTEGRITY NETWORK — The Water Integrity Network (WIN), formed in 2006, aims to fight corruption in the water sector. It stimulates anti-corruption activities in the water sector locally, nationally and globally. It promotes solutions-oriented action and coalition-building between civil society, the private and public sectors, media and governments.

WATER MISSIONS INTERNATIONAL — Water Missions International is a nonprofit Christian engineering organization providing sustainable safe water and sanitation solutions for people in developing countries and disaster areas. Safe water is the source of life. It is the foundation for health, education and viable economies. Through the generous support of individuals, churches, our corporate partners and many others, Water Missions International has brought relief and hope to more than 2.4 million people across the globe.

WATER PARTNERS INTERNATIONAL (WATER.ORG) — WaterPartners International is a U.S.-based nonprofit organization committed to providing safe drinking water and sanitation to people in developing countries. Working in partnership with donors and local communities, we have helped thousands of people develop accessible, sustainable, community-level water supplies. WaterPartners not only offers traditional, grant-funded programs, but is also harnessing the power of micro-finance to address the world water crisis.

WATER SUPPLY AND SANITATION COLLABORATIVE COUNCIL — WSSCC, together with its Members, staff, partners and donors, strives to achieve this vision. Such a vision is centered upon a belief that sanitation, hygiene and water supply coverage is a universal human right; that people and communities are catalysts of change and can be the focus of transformative action; and that the impact of sound sanitation and hygiene will positively benefit people's health, dignity, security, livelihoods, as well economic status.

WATERSTEP — Since 2001, WaterStep staff members and volunteers have been distributing and installing water treatment systems for use in developing communities. WaterStep seeks to prevent waterborne illness with truly sustainable solutions by training local people, solving problems creatively in the field, and improving developing communities' self-sufficiency.

WATER SUPPLY AND SANITATION COLLABORATIVE COUNCIL — Founded 1990 "through a mandate by the UN General Assembly to maintain the momentum of the International Drinking Water Supply and Sanitation Decade (1981-1990) . Enhances international "collaboration in the water supply and sanitation sector," especially regarding services for poor people. Members are some 2,000 professionals from over 140 countries.

WELL RESOURCE CENTER — The WELL website is a focal point for providing access to information about water, sanitation and environmental health and related issues in developing and transitional countries. Follow our INTERNATIONAL YEAR OF SANITATION link to go directly to our knowledge and information products concerning sanitation.

WORLD BUSINESS COUNCIL FOR SUSTAINABLE DEVELOPMENT — Founded 1995 through a merger of the Business Council for Sustainable Development and the World Industry Council for the Environment, the latter an initiative of the International Chamber of Commerce. "A coalition of some 150 international companies united by a shared commitment to sustainable development, i.e., environmental protection, social equity, and economic growth." Purposes are "to be the leading business advocate" on issues connected with the environment and sustainable development; participate in policy development; share leading-edge best practices; and contribute to developing countries and nations in transition. Themes are trade and environment; natural resources; innovation and technology; climate and energy; ecoefficiency; sustainability through the market; corporate social responsibility; exploring future global scenarios; and advancing a global compact in which business would embrace a set of core principles on labor standards, human rights, and environmental practices. Members of the Council are companies from some 30 countries and 20 major industrial sectors. WBCSD has national councils and partner organizations throughout the world.

WORLD COMMISSION ON DAMS — Established in 1998, the WCD was a "focused, independent think tank set up and financed by aid agencies, industry, governments, and NGOs to look at the good, the bad, and the ugly impacts of dams around the world." It disbanded with issuance of its final report in November 2000, Dams and Development: A New Framework for Decision-Making (published by Earthscan, London). From 2001-2003, UNEP conducted a follow-up effort, the Dams and Development Project (DDP).

WORLD HEALTH ORGANIZATION — WATER, SANITATION, AND, HYGIENE — Our aim is the reduction of water- and waste-related disease and the optimization of the health benefits of sustainable water and waste management. Our objectives are to 1) To support the health sector in effectively addressing water- and waste-related disease burden and in engaging others in its reduction, and 2) To assist non-health sectors in understanding and acting on the health impacts of their actions.

WORLD TOILET ORGANIZATION — World Toilet Organization (WTO) is a global non-profit organization committed to improving toilet and sanitation conditions worldwide. WTO is also one of the few organizations to focus on toilets instead of water, which receives more attention and resources under the common subject of sanitation. Founded in 2001 with 15 members, it now has 235 member organizations in 58 countries working towards eliminating the toilet taboo and delivering sustainable sanitation.

WORLD RESOURCES INSTITUTE — WRI focuses on the intersection of the environment and socio-economic development. We go beyond research to put ideas into action, working globally with governments, business, and civil society to build transformative solutions that protect the earth and improve people's lives.

WORLD WATER COUNCIL—The "international water policy think tank" created in response to a recommendation of the 1992 United Nations Conference on Environment and Development. Mission is to "promote awareness of critical water issues at all levels, including the highest decision-making level, to facilitate efficient conservation, protection, development, planning, management, and use of water in all its dimensions on an environmentally sustainable basis for the benefit of all life on earth." Activities include policy development; organizing meetings, including a triennial WWC Forum; monitoring the WWC's World Water Vision; and establishing a World Commission on Water, Peace, and Security. Members of WWC are some 300 organizations in 40 countries.

WSSCC—The Collaborative Council exists under a mandate from the United Nations. It is governed by a multi-stakeholder steering committee elected by the Collaborative Council's members, combining the authority of the UN with the flexibility of an NGO and the legitimacy of a membership organisation. WSSCC focuses exclusively on those people around the world who currently lack water and sanitation, with all its policies and work aimed only to serve those people. The Collaborative Council has a special interest in sanitation and hygiene and emphasizes the need to view water, sanitation and hygiene (WASH) as an inseparable trinity for development.

WWF INTERNATIONAL WATER STEWARDSHIP—From the United Nations to rural communities to corporate boardrooms, water issues are on the agenda as never before. WWF helps governments and businesses work together to better manage this essential resource.

*****

Welcoming the stranger.
Example: Agencies in Texas and NY where workers are able to help welcome the immigrants arriving from Central America:

CATHOLIC CHARITIES OF DALLAS, INC.
9461 LBJ Freeway, Suite 100, Dallas, TX 75243. (214) 634-7182 . Representation in removal proceedings for detained and non-detained cases within Dallas area. Will represent aliens in Asylum cases. Does not provide representation for aliens detained at the Big Spring facility, Eden, or Oklahoma.

HUMAN RIGHTS INITIATIVE OF NORTH TEXAS, INC.
2801 Swiss Avenue, Dallas, TX 75204 (214) 855-0520. Will only represent

aliens in the Dallas Immigration Court. Will represent aliens in asylum cases. Will represent juveniles. Will NOT provide representation in detention facilities.

JUSTICE FOR OUR NEIGIIBORS DFW.
North-Central Region, 422 Church Street, Grapevine, TX 76051 (817) 310-3820. www.jfondfw.org . Only represents clients at the Dallas Immigration Court. Will represent aliens in asylum cases.

UNITED NEIGHBORHOOD ORGANIZATION (UNO).
8660 Montana, Ste. I, El Paso, TX 79925. (915) 775-1161. Will not represent aliens in asylum or refugee cases. May charge a nominal fee.

IMMIGRANT HOPE - BROOKLYN, NY, INC.
6501 6th Ave, Brooklyn, NY 11220 (718) 745-7702. Adjustment of status, Consular Processing, Deferred Action for childhood arrivals, Family-based petitions, Naturalization/Citizenship, Temporary Protected Status, Violence Against Women petitions.

HANAC COMMUNITY SERVICES CENTER
Immigration Programs (Harlem Office), 127 W. 127th Street, Room 219, New York, NY 10027. Deferred Action for Childhood Arrivals, Naturalization/Citizenship, Removal hearings, Special Immigrant Juvenile Status, Violence Against Women Act. (212) 996-3949.

*****

Clothing the Naked:
Example: Websites about thrift shops that provide inexpensive clothing across USA:

http://www.thethriftshopper.com/
http://www.goodwill.org
http://www.salvationarmyusa.org/

Example: Website about free clothing in Alaska
(where it is really cold!):

CATHOLIC SOCIAL SERVICES/ ST. FRANCIS HOUSE.
3603721 East 20th Ave., Anchorage, AK
http://www.ccalaska.org. Food pantry and clothing closet.

*****

Visiting the sick:
Example: Agencies that manage hospice care for very ill patients, in one part of New Jersey:
NJPCO Members Hospices Serving Somerset County
(http://www.njhospice.org)

ATLANTIC HOME CARE AND HOSPICE (973) 379-8440
CARE ALTERNATIVES (908) 931-9080
CENTER FOR HOPE HOSPICE AND PALLIATIVE CARE (908) 889-7780
COMMUNITY CARE HOSPICE (908) 725-9355
COMPASSIONATE CARE HOSPICE (908) 526-2600
EMBRACING HOSPICE CARE (723) 9742545
GENTIVA HEALTHCARE (723) 562-8800
GRACE HEALTHCARE SERVICES (866) 447-0246
HAVEN HOSPICE (723) 321-7769
HOMESIDE HOSPICE (723) 381-3444
HOSPICE COMFORT CARE OF NJ (201) 437-7070
HUNTERDON HOSPICE (973) 788-6600
PRINCETON HEALTHCHARE SYSTEM HOSPICE (609) 497-4900
ROBERT WOOD JOHNSON VISITING NURSES HOSPICE (723) 743-4643
SAINT BARNABAS HOSPICE AND PALLIATIVE CARE CENTER (973) 322-4800
SERENITY HOSPICE CARE (609) 227-2400
SOMERSET HILLS HOSPICE (908) 766-0180
THE MARTIN AND EDITH STEIN HOSPICE (723) 227-1212
VNA OF MERCER COUNTY (609) 695-3461
VNA OF CENTRAL JERSEY (723) 695-4640
VITAS INNOVATIVE HOSPICE (723) 389-0066

*****

Visiting the imprisoned:
Example: Websites about prison minstries across the U.S.A.

http://www.prisonministry.net/directory/categories/%20cpminist/index.htm#sthash.GsnU0wxE.dpuf
http://www.cofchrist.org/peace/PrisonMinistry.pdf
http://hopeaglow.com/prison_ministry.htm
http://www.soulwinning.info/books/prison_ministry/toc.htm

Appendix C
Altruism and the Human Brain

1. amygdala
2. anterior cingulate cortex
3. brain stem
4. cerebellum
5. frontal gyrus/lobe/cortex
6. fusiform gyrus
7. hippocampus
8. hypothalamus
9. insula
10. orbitofrontal cortex
11. parietal lobe/cortex
12. posterior cingulate cortex
13. posterior medial cortex
14. periaqueductal
15. prefrontal cortex
16. premotor areas
17. temporal lobe/cortex
18. temporo-parietal junction
19. supramarginal gyrus: intersection of the frontal, parietal and temporal lobes

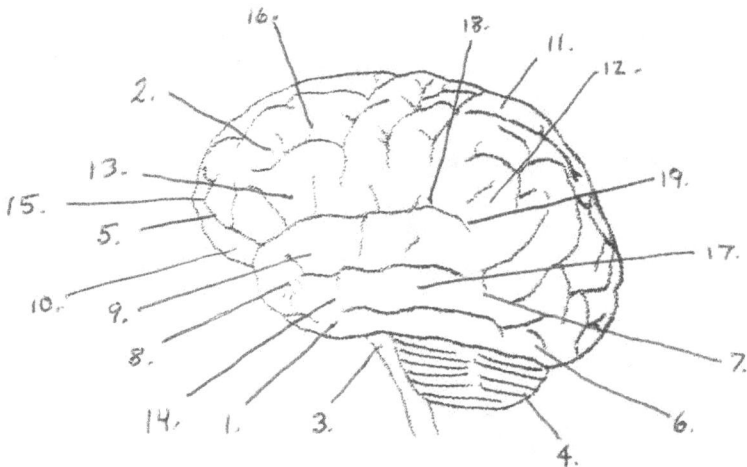

List of References

About OCD. (2014). Yale School of Medicine. Retrieved from http://medicine.yale.edu/psychiatry/ocd/aboutocd/index.aspx#page1.

Alcott, L.M. (1868). *Little Women*. Boston: Roberts Brothers.

American Psychiatric Association. (2013). *Diagnostic and Statistical Manual of Mental Disorders* (5th Edition). Washington DC: American Psychiatric Association.

Batson, C.D., Dyck, J.L., Brandt, J.R., Batson, J.G., Powell, A.L., McMaster, M.R. & Griffitt, C. (1988). Five studies testing two new egoistic alternatives to the empathy-altruism hypothesis. *Journal of Personality and Social Psychology*, 55 (1), 52-77.

Bauer, D.J., vanOyen Witvliet, C. & Vanderlaan, K.L. (2001). The forgiving attitude: How individual differences influence emotions during imagery of offenders. *Program of the 73rd Annual Meeting of the Midwestern Psychological Association*, May 3-5, 2001, 169.

Baumgartner, T.G., Gotte, L., Gugler. R. & Fehr, E. (2012). The mentalizing network orchestrates the impact of parochial altruism on social norm enforcement. *Human Brain Mapping*, 33 (6), 1452-1469.

Baytiyeh. H. & Pfaffman, J. (2010). Open source software: A community of altruists. *Computers in Human Behavior*, 26 (6), 1345-1354.

Beadle, J.N., Tranel, D., Cohen, N.J. & Duff, M.C. (2013). Empathy in hippocampal amnesia. *Frontiers in Psychology*, 4 (March 22, 2013), Article 69.

Beauregard, M. & O'Leary, D. (2007). *The spiritual brain: A neuroscientist's case for the existence of the soul*. New York: Harper One.

Beck, A. (2013) *Cognitive behavior therapy*. Retrieved from http://www.beckinstitute.org/what-is-cognitive-behavioral-therapy/About-CBT/252/).

Bernt, F.M. (1989). Being religious and being altruistic: A study of college service volunteers. *Personality and Individual Differences*, 10 (6), 663-669.

Bradley, A.C. (1901). *A Commentary on Tennyson's in Memoriam*. London: Macmillan and Co.

Burks, D. J., Youll, L.K. & Durtschi, J.P. (2012). The empathy-altruism association and its relevance to health care professions. *Social Behavior and Personality*, 40 (3), 395-400.

Buss, E. (2013). *Six ways to serve the neighbor*. (Unpublished manuscript).

Casey-Acevedo, K. & Bakken, T. (2002). Visiting women in prison: Who visits and who cares. *Journal of Offender Rehabilitation*, 34 (3), 67-83.

Chang, H.H. & Chuang, S. (2011). Social capital and individual motivations on knowledge sharing: Participant involvement as a moderator. *Information & Management*, 48 (1), 9-18.

Cherry, K . (2014). *Cognitive-Behavioral Therapy*. Retrieved from http://www.about.psychology.com/od/psychotherapy/a/cbt.htm.

Cheung, C. (2006). Experiential learning strategies for promoting adolescents' voluntarism in Hong Kong. *Child & Youth Care Forum*, 35 (1), 57-78.

Darley, J.M. & Batson, C.D. (1973). From Jerusalem to Jericho: A study of situational and dispositional variables in helping behavior. *Journal of Personality and Social Psychology*, 27 (1), 100-108.

Dickens, C, (1938). *A Christmas Carol*. Great Britain: John C. Winston Co.

Dostoevsky, F. (1880). *The Brothers Karamasov*. Russia: Pevear & Volokhonsky.

Edlefsen, M.S. & Olson C.M. (2002). Perspectives of volunteers in emergency feeding programs on hunger, its causes, and solutions. *Journal of Nutrition Education and Behavior*, 34 (2), 93-99.

Farrow, T.F.D., Zheng, Y., Wilkinson, I.D., Spence, S.A. Deakin, J.F.,Tarrier, N., Griffiths, P.D. & Woodruff, P.W.R. (2001). Investigating the functional anatomy of empathy and forgiveness. *NeuroReport: For rapid communication of neuroscience research*, 12 (11), 2433-2438.

Freberg, L. (2010). *Discovering biological psychology*. (Second Edition). Belmont, CA: Wadsworth.

Gamblers Anonymous (2014). *Recovery program*. Retrieved from www.gamblersanonymous.org.

Gardner, H., Czikszentmihalyi, M. & Damon, W. (2001). *Good work: When excellence and ethics meet*. New York: Basic Books.

Goleman, D. (2006). *Social intelligence: The new science of human relationships*. New York: Bantam Dell.

Grossman, J.B. & Garry, E.M. (1997). Mentoring: A proven delinquency prevention strategy. *OJJDP Juvenile Justice Bulletin*, 7. (US Department of Justice DOJ).

Guo, X., Zheng, L., Wang, H., Zhu, L., Li, J., Wang, Q., Dienes, Z. & Yang. Z. (2013). Exposure to violence reduces empathic responses to other's pain. *Brain and Cognition*, 82 (2), 187-191.

Ha-Brookshire, J.E. & Hodges, N.N. (2009). Socially responsible consumer behavior? Exploring used clothing donation behavior. *Clothing & Textiles Research Journal*, 27 (3), 179-196.

Haidt, J. (2012). *The righteous mind: Why good people are divided by politics and religion*. New York: Pantheon Books.

Hoexter, M.Q., Dougherty, D.D., Shavitt, R.G., D'Alcante, C.C., Duran, F.L., Lopes, A.C., Diniz, J.B., Batistuzzo, M.C., Evans, K.C., Bressan, R. A., Busatto, G. F. & Miguel, E.C. (2013). Differential prefrontal gray matter correlates of treatment response to fluoxetine or cognitive-behavioral therapy in obsessive-compulsive disorder. *Neuropsychopharmacology*, 23 (7), 569-580.

Holy Bible. Retrieved from http://www.biblegateway.com/passage/?search=Genesis+9&version=NIV

Huffmeijer, R., Alink, L.R. A., Tops, M., Bakermans-Kranenburg, M.J. & Van Ijzendoorn, M.H. (2012). Asymmetric frontal brain activity and parental rejection predict altruistic behavior: Moderation of oxytocin effects. *Cognitive, Affective & Behavioral Neuroscience*, 12 (2), 382-392.

Hugo, V. (1862). *Les Miserables*. Paris, France: A. Lacroix, Verboeckhoven & Cie.

Huyser, C., van den Heuvel, O.A., Wolters, L.H., de Haan, E., Boer, F. & Veltman, D.J. (2013). Increased orbital frontal gray matter volume after cognitive behavioral therapy in paediatric obsessive compulsive disorder. *The World Journal of Biological Psychiatry*, 14 (4), 319-331.

James, H. (1881). *The portrait of a lady*. Boston: MacMillan.

James, W. (1902). *Varieties of religious experiences*. London: Longmans Green.

Keller, H. (1927). *My religion*. NY: Doubleday, Page.

Keyes, C.L.M. & Haidt, J. (2003). *Flourishing: Positive psychology and the life well-lived*. Washington DC: American Psychological Association.

Klein, J.T. (1998). *The power of service: A Swedenborgian approach to social issues in the 21st century*. San Francisco: J. Appleseed & Co.

Krueger, F., Parasuraman, R., Moody, L., Twieg, P., de Visser, E., McCabe, K., O'Hara, M. & Lee, M.R. (2013). Oxytocin selectively increases perceptions of harm for victims but not the desire to punish offenders of criminal offenses. *Social Cognitive and Affective Neuroscience*, 8 (5), 494-498.

LaBouff, J.P. Rowatt, W.C., Johnson, M.K., Tsang, J. & Willerton, G.M. (2012). Humble person are more helpful than less humble persons: Evidence from three studies. *The Journal of Positive Psychology*, 7 (1), 16-29.

Lamm, C., Batson, C.D. & Decety, J. (2007). The neural substrate of human empathy: Effects of perspective-taking and cognitive appraisal. *Journal of Cognitive Neuroscience*, 19 (1), 42-58.

Lewis, C.S. (1992). *Readings for meditation and reflection: The Christian view of suffering*. New York: HarperCollins.

McCann, K.J, Twomey, J.E., Caldwell, D., Soave, R., Fontaine, L.A. & Lester, B.M. (2010). Service used by perinatal substance-users with child welfare involvement: A descriptive study. *Harm Reduction Journal*, 7, Article 19.

Meyer, M.L., Masters, C.L., Ma, Y., Wang, C., Shi, Z., Eisenberger, N.I. & Han, S.H. (2013). Empathy for the social suffering of friends and strangers recruits distinct patterns of brain activation. *Social Cognitive and Affective Neuroscience, 8* (4), 446-454.

Mt. Saint Peter Parish. (2014). *Visiting the imprisoned.* Retrieved from http://www.mountsaintpeter.org/pages/liturgy/cwm/imprisioned.html

Myers, D.G. (1992). *The pursuit of happiness: Discovering the pathway to fulfillment, well-being, and enduring personal joy.* New York: HarperCollins.

NIH. (2014). Islamic culture and the medical arts: Hospitals. *National Institute of Health.* Retrieved from https://www.nlm.nih.gov/exhibition/islamic_medical/islamic_12.html

Nierenberg, D. (2014). *101 organizations to watch in 2014.* Retrieved from http://foodtank.org/news/2014/01/one-hundred-one-organizations-to-watch-in-2014.

Newman, B.M. & Newman, P. R. (2012). *Development through life (11th Edition).* Belmont, CA: Wadsworth.

Oz, S. (2014) *GlobalPost: How to console a friend in prison.* Retrieved from http://everydaylife.globalpost.com/console-friend-prison-8502.html.

Peterson, C. & Seligman, M. (2004). *Character strengths and virtues.* Oxford, England: Oxford University Press.

Peterson, C. (2006). *A primer in positive psychology.* Oxford, England: Oxford University Press.

Piferi, R.L., Jobe, R.L. & Jones, W.H. (2006). Giving to others during national tragedy: The effects of altruistic and egoistic motivations on long-term giving. *Journal of Social and Personal Relationships, 23* (1), 171-184.

Post, S.G., Johnson, B., McCullough, M.E. & Schloss, J.P. (2003). *Research on altruism and love.* Philadelphia: Templeton Foundation Press.

Post, S.G. (2003). *Unlimited love: Altruism, compassion and service.* Philadelphia: Templeton Foundation Press.

Praetorius, R.T. & Machtmes, K. (2005). Volunteer crisis hotline counselors: An expression of spirituality. *Social Work & Christianity*, 32 (2), 116-132.

Pugh, E.J., Smith, S. & Salter, P. (July 19, 2010) Offering spiritual support to dying patients and their families through a chaplaincy service. *NursingTimes*, (28) Retrieved from http://www.nursingtimes.net/nursing-practice/clinical-zones/end-of-life-and-palliative-care/offering-spiritual-support-to-dying-patients-and-their-families-through-a-chaplaincy-service/5017364.article.

Rangan, R. K., O'Connor, L.E., Berry, J.W., Stiver, D.J., Choi, K.W., Li, Y., Ark, W. & Hanson, R. (2013). Compassion, altruism, contemplative practices and psychological well-being. *Conference Proceedings for APA Convention*. doi: 10.1037/e602652013-001.

Salvation Army. (2014). Retrieved from http://satruck.org/

Schnall, S., Roper, J. & Fessler, D.M.T. (2010). Elevation leads to altruistic behavior. *Psychological Science*, 21 (3), 315-320.

Seligman, M.E.P. (1993). *What you can change...and what you can't*. New York: Fawcett Columbine.

Seligman, M.E.P. (1998). *Learned optimism: How to change your mind and your life*. New York: Free Press.

Sew Much Comfort. (2014). Retrieved from http://www.sewmuchcomfort.org/

Shaw, S.M. (2012). *Paradise Misplaced*. West Chester, PA: Swedenborg Foundation.

Silani, G., Lamm, C.C., Ruff & Singer, T. (2013). Right supramarginal gyrus is crucial to overcome emotional egocentricity bias in social judgments. *Journal of Neuroscience*, 33 (39), 15466-15476.

Silverman, R. (1994). *Light in my Darkness*. West Chester, PA: Swedenborg Foundation.

Simon-Thomas, E.R., Godzik, J., Castle, E., Antonenko, O., Ponz, A., Kogan, A. & Keltner, D. (2012), An fMRI study of caring vs self-focus during induced compassion and pride. *Social Cognitive and Affective*

Neuroscience, 7 (6), 635-648.

Snyder, C.R. (1994). *The psychology of hope*. New York: The Free Press.

Snyder, C.R. & Lopez, S.J. (Eds.) (2002). *Handbook of positive psychology*. Oxford, England: Oxford University Press.

Soles4Souls. (2014). *Our mission*. Retrieved from http://soles4souls.org/our-mission.

Sorokin, P.A. (1954). *The ways and power of love: Types, factors, and techniques of moral transformation*. Philadelphia: Templeton Foundation Press.

Starr, M. (June 25, 2013). *'Bridge of Life' projects messages to prevent suicides*. CNET.com. Retrieved from http://www.cnet.com/news/.

Strobel, M., Tumasjan, A., Sporrle, M. & Welpe, I.M. (2013). The future starts today: How future focus promotes organizational citizenship behaviors. *Human Relations*, 66 (6), 829-856.

Suarez-Orozco, C. Birman, D., Casas, J.M., Nakamura, N., Tummala-Narra, P. & Zarate, M. (2011). *APA Presidential Task Force on Immigration*. Retrieved from http://www.apa.org/topics/immigration/report.aspx?item=14.

Swedenborg, E. (1947). *Charity*. London: Swedenborg Society.

Swedenborg, E. (1978). *Heaven and Hell*. New York: Swedenborg Foundation.

Swedenborg, E. (1978). *The spiritual diary*. New York: Swedenborg Foundation.

Swedenborg, E. (1980). *Apocalypse explained*. New York: Swedenborg Foundation.

Swedenborg, E. (1980). *Conjugial love*. New York: Swedenborg Foundation.

Swedenborg, E. (1984). *Arcana coelestia*. New York: Swedenborg Foundation.

Swedenborg, E. (1984). *True Christian religion*. New York: Swedenborg Foundation.

Sweitzer, H.F. & King, M.A. (2004). *The successful internship: Transformation and empowerment in experiential learning*. Belmont, CA: Thomson.

Tennyson, A. Baron (1896). *The works of Alfred Lord Tennyson*. New York: Macmillan.

United Nations Refugee Agency. (2014). Retrieved from http://www.unrefugees.org.

Vanderlaan, K.L., Bauer, D.J. & vanOyen Witvliet, C. (2000). To forgive or not to forgive: Emotional costs and benefits. *Program of the 72nd Annual Meeting of the Midwestern Psychological Association*, May 4-6, 2000, 204.

Van Dusen, W. (2000). *Uses: A way of personal and spiritual growth*. West Chester, PA: Swedenborg Foundation.

Vecina, M.K. & Fernando, C. (2013). Volunteering and well-being: Is pleasure-based rather than pressure-based prosocial motivation that which is related to positive effects? *Journal of Applied Social Psychology*, 43 (4), 870-878.

Waytz, A., Zaki, J. & Mitchell, J.P. (2012). Response of dorsomedial prefrontal cortex predicts altruistic behavior. *The Journal of Neuroscience*, 32 (22), 7646-7650.

Weil, K. (2013). Hope: Mission possible. *Monitor on Psychology*, 44 (9), 42-45.

Wilson, J. (1992). *Lawrence of Arabia: The authorized biography of T.E. Lawrence*. New York: Collier Books/Simon & Schuster.

World Water Council (2014). *Water for the ages*. Retrieved from http://waterfortheages.org/international-water-organizations.

Yates, M. (1995). Community service and identity development in adolescence. *Dissertation Abstracts International: Section B: The Sciences and Engineering*, 56 (5-B), 2908.

Yorke, C. (1990). A psychoanalytic approach to the understanding of shame. *Sigmund Freud House Bulletin*, 14 (2), 14-28.

About the Author

Dr. Soni Soneson Werner is a Swedenborgian Developmental Psychologist. She currently teaches psychology and interpersonal communication skills at Bryn Athyn College to undergraduates and graduate theological students.

Soni is also the author of Searching for *Mary Magdalene: Her Story of Awareness, Acceptance and Action* and *Growth of the Female Mind: Sincerity and Severity*. She is married to Dr. Neil Werner and they have two grown daughters.